In Search
of a Lovely
Moment

In Search of a Lovely Moment

Roger Breland

THOMAS NELSON PUBLISHERS
Nashville

Published in Nashville, Tennessee, by Thomas Nelson, Inc., and distributed in Canada by Lawson Falle, Ltd., Cambridge, Ontario.

Scripture quotations unless otherwise noted are from the NEW KING JAMES VERSION of the Bible. Copyright © 1979, 1980, 1982, Thomas Nelson, Inc., Publishers.

Bible verses marked TLB are taken from The Living Bible (Wheaton, IL: Tyndale, 1971) and are used by permission.

Lyrics for "My Tribute" were printed with permission of Communique Music. Copyright © 1971, COMMUNIQUE' MUSIC (ASCAP) (Administered by Copyright Management, Inc.) 1102 17th Avenue South, Nashville, TN. All rights reserved.

Library of Congress Cataloging-in-Publication Data

Breland, Roger.
    In search of a lovely moment / Roger Breland.
        p.   cm.
    ISBN 0-8407-3014-4 (pbk.)
    1. Truth (Musical group)   2. Gospel musicians—United States-
-Biography.   3. Contemporary Christian music—United States—History
and criticism.   I. Title.
ML421.T78B7   1991
782.25'092'2—dc20
[B]   90-24414
                                                          CIP
                                                          MN

Printed in the United States of America
1 2 3 4 5 6 7 — 95 94 93 92 91 90

For twenty years I have crisscrossed the country missing birthdays, anniversaries, basketball games, piano recitals, school plays, and mostly home. But God has graciously blessed me with a wonderful wife and three fine sons. They have prayerfully supported me and allowed me the freedom to do God's will for my life.

John, you brought real joy to our little home in a rural town in Alabama. I can hardly believe you're now grown and married to a beautiful woman, Tracy. The years have flown by, but they have drawn us closer and have given us much joy. I can still remember the Sunday morning when, as a seven year old, you accepted Jesus Christ in one of our concerts. I am so proud of you, and I love you.

Jason, our middle son. You arrived with a unique freshness, with mounds of creativity, and with a desire to conquer the unconquerable. I remember one day asking you if you wanted to be in TRUTH when you grew up and you abruptly said, "NO, I want to direct TRUTH when I grow up!" You just might too! I love your desire to make things happen. You're a gift from God.

Jeremy, you make me smile! Carefree, sloppy t-shirt, hole in your jeans, can never find your shoes. I remember when you used to fall asleep during our family devotions and when you shared the Christmas story on our TV special. You are God's surprise to your Mom and me.

And Linda, I saw you my first day at college, gave you a Valentine the following February 14, dated you for three years, and have spent every year since thanking God for allowing you to be my best friend, prayer partner, and wife. My love and respect for you grows year after year as we have weathered storm after storm. You've been a wife without a husband most days, raised three sons, and prayed for me and TRUTH. I can't imagine God being so good to me. I love you with all my heart and have joy in the thought that we will spend eternity together.

Yours and His,
JRB

Contents

Foreword
By Jay Strack

In the last twenty years amid the noise of the 70s and 80s, there has been a voice attempting to turn young lives around. Sometimes this voice is heard in a high school stadium, on the beach, on a college campus, at a large youth convention, or in the 11 o'clock Sunday morning service in a local church. This voice is a contemporary Christian musical group called TRUTH. I know of no other ministry in the past twenty years that has turned as many young people from darkness to light, and I know of no other ministry in the last twenty years that has produced more individuals for full-time Christian service. The phenomena of this group is that like a precious stone, every facet seems to reflect the glory of God. I have known Roger Breland and the various personnel of TRUTH for almost twenty years, and I am a TRUTH fan. Let me speak first from a personal perspective, then as a pastor, and finally as a parent.

One of the reasons for my gratitude for TRUTH is the role that they played in my life as a young

Christian. Almost nineteen years go, I gave my life to Christ, and I found Him to be everything that He promised to be. He gave me power which I had never experienced and a purpose for my existence. However, I was still struggling the first few months with shaking off some old habits, and in particular, some old attitudes. When an individual has been delivered from the alcohol and drug scene, Friday and Saturday nights are particularly tough.

On a Saturday night, when the Devil and his forces were beating me up in the back alley of my mind and when certain lusts were raging within my body, I was invited to a TRUTH concert. For the first time, I experienced the power of Christian music. For many years, I had been in bondage with the power of the world's music, but at a critical time in my life, I saw sharp young men and young women sold out to Jesus with musical talent as good as any group I had ever heard. This time the message was a positive one and exalted Jesus. That night, I rededicated my life, and the young girl who went with me to the concert is now my wife. I am convinced that the music of TRUTH enabled me to go forward in my Christian walk.

Every pastor struggles with helping his young people find alternatives to the music of MTV while at the same time not offending the older congregation. TRUTH has the versatility and the spirit to accomplish such a difficult task. Through the years, this group has been able to turn a stadium into a sanctuary and a civic center into a cathedral. Oftentimes as a pastor, we bring in groups in an effort to reach young people, but by their appearance and attitude, these groups are more worldly than the world. Unfortunately, some groups become an echo of society rather than a voice for God. Thank God for a group that epitomizes in appearance and attitude that they are servants of Christ.

Every parent is rightfully concerned about the glitter of the "scene" that entices so many young people. I have stated many times that parents should not prohibit without providing a substitute. The music of TRUTH has been such a substitute for thousands of parents. My own daughters prefer to listen to the music of TRUTH over that of anyone on the radio today, and I am thrilled to see that they are listening to music with a Scriptural message.

The commitment of any group will never be any greater than the commitment of its leader. To understand the success of TRUTH, you need to look no farther than its founder and leader, Roger Breland. An accomplished church musician, Roger has the ability to be geared to the times but anchored to the Rock. It can be said of Roger in both his professional and personal life that his fruit remains.

Roger has raised three wonderful sons who love the Lord and are committed to the ministry and to serving the Lord. His wife, Linda, is a gracious and warm lady who ministers to the TRUTH family and to countless others, both in her local church and as she accompanies Roger in concerts from time to time.

Of the more than 300 young people who have performed in TRUTH through the last twenty years, some 95 percent are in the ministry today. TRUTH is seeing lives changed in the name of Jesus around the world today, and I believe a great deal of their success is because Roger Breland walks with God.

Although the quote "Music has two purposes; one, to bring glory to God, and the other, to lift our spirits" has been attributed to Handel, it could just as well have been written today to describe the music of TRUTH. I am proud to count Roger Breland and TRUTH among my personal friends, and I believe THE BEST IS YET TO COME.

Lovely Moments

"It was a lovely moment," the woman said.

As I listened, I thought, *We do speak of moments in time, don't we?* As if they are isolated from everything else. We use such terms to describe the highlight of a concert, a decision in an athletic event, or a poignant conversation. Sometimes we speak of joyous moments or empty occasions or instances when we've failed or been misunderstood.

I decided to search for the lovely moments in life—a look back at those special times that have made life so rich and delightful—and to put those moments into a book. In my preparation to write *In Search of a Lovely Moment,* my wife, Linda, and I reread old letters and pored over journals.

Now we're ready to share some of these lovely moments, to show them just as we viewed them then. When they happened, we didn't always know they were lovely moments. We sometimes called them unlovely, painful, hard, sad.

Looking back we realize that God has been at work every second of our lives. Events we considered unlovely at the time, God has used to give us wisdom, teach us compassion, and turn us from things that don't please Him. Most of all, through all these moments, God was drawing us closer to Him and to each other.

And we're still learning that every struggle can be a lovely moment if only we're willing to search for God's will and wait for the loveliness to reveal itself.

Chapter 1

Moment of Waiting

"I want to travel with a group. I want to challenge people, and to communicate the gospel through music and—"

"Roger," friends challenged, "you need to stay right where you are. You've got a good job at Spring Hill Baptist, and you're serving the Lord. What more do you want?"

"I want to go on the road."

"You can do everything you want to do in Mobile," they'd say. "Road life looks glamorous, but it's tough."

I had a dream, a vision: I wanted to form a group of singers and instrumentalists to go on the road full-time. But everyone I talked to about the idea thought I was crazy. My best friends didn't understand. My mother decided I was a little confused. And my wife thought I was wrong.

How does a man cope with all the negative voices

when he thinks God is speaking to him? What does he do when he wants to honor God, but he has no support from the people he loves the most?

If I had really thought this was just a whim of mine, I would have quit at the first word of opposition. But I was convinced this dream, this vision, would honor God. I had memorized a verse as a young boy that helped me at critical times like this.

When I was ten years old, I attended Vacation Bible School at Mount Calvary Baptist Church. I worked hard that week learning some verses to receive a little red Bible. I memorized Matthew 28:19–20, some of the last words Jesus spoke before He went into heaven after His resurrection: "Go therefore and make disciples of all the nations," Jesus told His disciples. He said to baptize them in the name of the Father and of the Son and of the Holy Spirit, and teach them to observe all things that He had commanded. And then He said, "Lo, I am with you always, even to the end of the age."

I have had little doubt through the years that one of Christ's primary missions for me is to share the gospel with anyone I meet, and I've been encouraged to know that He promised to be always with me. I knew that my desire to go on the road would enable me to tell others about Christ, so I was confident that He would open the door to go. God couldn't fail—though I did begin to wonder if people could get in His way. For the moment I simply had to wait. Now, I have never enjoyed waiting. But I'd rather wait than quit, especially if God's business is concerned, and I needed to wait until both Linda and I were ready.

I could move ahead in life without most people's

approval—even the approval of my parents whom I loved and trusted—but I couldn't move ahead without Linda's support. She had always supported me before, through every tough time, through moments of indecision and uncertainty.

When I first saw Linda, we were both standing in the registration line for freshman classes at Troy State in Troy, Alabama. Oh! I was glad to be there. My father had driven me to school. I hardly looked back as he drove away, my mom at his side—in tears of course. But I had lived for the day I would get away from home. And it was finally here.

I'm not sure how long I'd been standing in that line—maybe one hour, maybe three. I'd never liked standing in long lines, and this was certainly the longest I had ever endured.

Hundreds of other students, all trying to look as if they knew where they were and what they were doing, surrounded me. In the heat of the large room, my clothes and my spirits were beginning to wilt. I was definitely feeling insecure and out of place. I wondered if everyone around me was feeling the same thing.

Suddenly, I spotted the most beautiful girl I'd ever seen. She was wearing a pink sundress that offset her Florida tan, her blond ponytail shone under the lights and above the blue eyes that were focused intently on the course schedule she was carefully developing. She looked crisp as early morning coolness and lovely—and very far away. I couldn't take my eyes off her.

Welcome to college! I thought. *I'd sure like to meet her.* But I was sure there was no way she would ever go out with me. My folks hadn't let me have a car to drive to college, and I didn't think any girl who looked that beautiful would consider going out with someone who didn't have a set of wheels.

She's probably dating the football players and wouldn't be interested in me anyway, I consoled myself, and I wrote her off, thinking I'd never see her again.

When I returned to campus with a car after the Christmas vacation, I took a long, deep breath, prayed very hard, and dialed her number.

She wasn't really sure who I was. A mutual friend had been telling her since September that I wanted to date her. Understandably, by January she had given up.

But she agreed to go out with me, and that January Sunday evening we went on our first date—to church. I was a member of the college choir there, and they were singing as we walked in late. They all smiled at me, a smile of congratulations that I had finally succeeded. In her gray and black striped suit with a little fur collar, she looked prettier than the first day I had seen her.

Our first Valentine's Day I sent her two cards. The first one was funny and signed "Your friend." The second one was serious and signed "Yours! John Roger Breland, 2 Samuel 22:33." Neither of us ever dated anyone else after that. Linda loves beautiful cards and has kept every Valentine I've ever sent her, including the first two. And I still enjoy giving them to her. She was—and is—the girl of my dreams. I graduated from Troy State in June of 1964, and we married on September 12, 1964.

Linda and I had high expectations for our marriage

because we had dated for almost three years and had experienced a wonderful relationship all through college.

Immediately after our wedding, Linda and I were to move to Opp so that I could begin work. I had accepted a job in Opp, Alabama, as a part-time church choir director and a high school choral director. Linda planned to commute to Troy State to finish her college degree. We didn't expect to have the *perfect* marriage—just something close to it.

How different reality was. I think Linda cried every day for the first year. At the time she didn't know why she was crying. I didn't know why she was crying either. She just cried.

Now we know that part of it was that I was young and overly committed to my career, determined to hit the home run every time I was at the plate. That fact plus Linda's long commutes to Troy State left us too little time together. We were actually together less than when we were dating!

A few weeks before the wedding, I went to Opp alone to find a place for us to live. I fell in love with the first house I visited. And I knew Linda would feel the same way. A couple with an upstairs garage apartment wanted to rent it at a price I could afford, so I arranged for us to move in—no hesitation.

The week before we married I drove Linda to Opp to introduce her to the people I'd be working with and to show her our new home. I couldn't wait to see her look of surprise.

And look of surprise it was.

Linda stared—first at the apartment, then at me.

I beamed. "Isn't it great, honey?"

She looked blank; then tears began to roll down her cheeks.

"You don't like it?"

Linda shook her head. "It's . . . it's—awful." I couldn't believe it.

She was right, of course. I looked around the room and noticed for the first time how tiny it was. The walls were dull and the floors were dusty. Paint flaked down from a stained spot on the ceiling where the water had once leaked through the roof. I wasn't quite sure what kind of place Linda would have chosen, but I knew this didn't fit the description.

"I'm sorry, Linda," I mumbled. "I wasn't really thinking."

"We'll be all right," Linda reassured me, though her words didn't sound very convincing.

"Once you're out of school and finances are better," I promised, "we'll get something better. A lot better."

"That's not important, Roger. I'm just glad we're together."

That's the way Linda was. As it turned out, we didn't have to live in the garage apartment. We found a furnished apartment that was much better, though still a far cry from the home of our dreams. But in this instance as in many others in our first years of marriage, Linda always came through. She came to support almost every crazy scheme I dreamed up—from living in a small apartment to save money, to my having the Spring Hill Singers perform for the America's Junior Miss pageant contestants. Linda's tenacious ability to love me in spite of myself, her ability to hang on and believe for both of us, always made home a place of refreshment and stability, a place from which I could safely look for new races to run and new mountains to climb.

Maybe that's why I couldn't believe that Linda didn't want to discuss or even listen to my vision to have a full-time ministry on the road.

~

The dream to go on the road was born during my second year as minister of music at Spring Hill Baptist in Mobile, Alabama. (We had moved to Mobile from Opp in August, 1967.) A group called the Spurrlows, led by a man named Thurlow Spurr, came to sing at my home church, First Baptist of Chickasaw, Alabama. It was the late 1960s, and a new sound had begun to revolutionize music in the churches in America—and to shock churches in the South. Traditional gospel music was being set to a soft pop/rock 'n' roll beat. Guitar, brass, and percussion were being used as choir accompaniment.

I had first heard the new sound in December of 1967, when a youth choir performed a musical called *Good News* at a youth convention I attended. After I returned from the convention, I bought the music for our youth choir to perform.

The music was exciting and the kids loved it. Because we were in the deep conservative South and I was uncertain how the parents would respond to the new sound, I tentatively introduced the contemporary music into our church—not much guitar the first year, the softest songs. Kids who had never participated in church began to come to choir rehearsals. The parents, thrilled to see their children's commitment and involvement, only encouraged us.

In the two years I had been at Spring Hill, the choir had grown from 7 members to 140 members. The group called themselves the Spring Hill Singers. A combination of the new music and my spending hours with them both during rehearsals and around their schools and Sunday school classes had motivated them to see that I was serious about music and about them. As they discovered their talent, their excitement flamed and their desire to perform increased.

Always hungry to learn more about contemporary music, I was ready to go anywhere I could hear it discussed or performed. So the night the Spurrlows came to First Baptist Church in Chickasaw, I was in the audience. And I witnessed one of the most powerful performances I had ever heard.

As I settled back into a pew, eight young singers walked in. I couldn't believe my eyes! The young women wore beautiful long blue gowns, and the men were elegant in black tuxedos. At one side of the auditorium sat the orchestra, and the singers were paired at microphones in the front. The harmony and style of their presentation were deeply moving, and in a few minutes the entire audience was awed, profoundly receptive to the testimonies that group members shared between numbers. For the first time I heard a gospel group use the contemporary sound throughout their performance.

"That sound, that style," I kept saying. I was mesmerized. At the close of the concert they sang a beautiful arrangement of "Have You Met Jesus?" Right then, a dream was born: I wanted to be a director of a group like the Spurrlows. More than wanted to be, from that time on I knew I had to be.

When I returned home that night, I couldn't stop talking about the group's performance. "Linda, I have to direct a group like that. Our kids could do it. I know they could." Although Linda could see my awe at the music I'd heard, she had little idea of the determination that had been sparked in me. I didn't organize a group like the Spurrlows right then, but every step I took with my own choir after that was motivated by that desire.

Groups similar to the Spurrlows began to form all over the country, and I soon began to hear more about them. The Continental Singers, ReGeneration, the New Hope Singers—they toured the country, and I invited some of the groups to sing at our church.

In high school I had sung in the church youth choir and played in the school band. Everyone I knew or had heard of usually chose one but not both areas of music. At the time I had been determined to find a way to combine the two, but I couldn't figure out how. As I listened to the new groups, I finally understood how to combine the big-band sound with a select group of singers who would perform Christian music. With my new idea of how to challenge the Spring Hill Singers and reach even more kids, I visited the band director of one of the larger high schools in Mobile one day and proposed a plan.

"Look," I said after I introduced myself and told him of my experience, "you've got a big band, and you set up a Christmas concert every year to showcase their talent. But you never have a large crowd. You attract a few grandparents and maybe a few hundred others.

"I've got this big choir of 140 to 160 kids who are trained and who want to sing."

"I know about your choir," he responded. "I've heard them at the mall. You do a good job with them."

"Okay, then, why don't we do something together? Why not invite my choir to be your guests for the band concert?" He didn't say much of anything, but I could tell he was thinking about my idea. So I plunged on.

"First, if we do this jointly, we're going to pull in three times more people. Maybe I'll be a guest conductor, or you can do it. We could do a patriotic package. You set up a 150-piece band, and I'll put a 140-voice choir behind them. We'll rival the Mormon Tabernacle Choir. In the middle of the program we'll let the American flag fall out of the ceiling. The people will come unglued." My new friend jumped to the edge of his chair.

"That's great! Let's do it!"

When I told our kids later, they became elated. We did the joint program for a packed house. When it came time for me to do Christmas music at the church and at the mall, I asked my friend if he wanted to do another joint program.

This time he didn't hesitate. We combined our energies and presented an outstanding musical program.

And that's how it worked. My philosophy was that I couldn't get a bunch of people excited just by rehearsing them—they had to have places and opportunities to perform. So I started thinking up new ways to showcase the kids. The performances generated support from the adults, and the kids were transformed.

Always, too, I bore in mind that the kids weren't just putting on a show. They were working *toward* something. Along with their musical goals, I wanted them to keep the focus on Jesus Christ. Forming and developing the Spring Hill Singers and Varsity brought everything together for me. For the first time I understood how to blend the big-band sound, a select group of singers, and the Christian faith into a ministry for Christ.

As requests for Spring Hill Singers performances began to come more frequently throughout the community, I noticed that we had a few kids who were gifted above the rest of the group. These young people needed a way to continue to develop their musical ability and a place to use it. *Take them on the road, Roger,* I thought. *Why not form your own traveling group?*

Why not, indeed? My desire to go on the road had only intensified in the months since the Spurrlow concert. The kids needed to be challenged. So, from the members of the choir, we formed an ensemble of fifteen people, both instrumentalists and vocalists, to travel and to give special performances. We called ourselves the Varsity.

Before we began to travel, we made a commitment to be in church every Sunday morning for the eight-fifteen worship service unless we were on summer tour. During the school year we toured on weekends.

And each summer we presented Summer Symphony with the Spring Hill Singers and Varsity at the municipal auditorium. Then we toured the Southwest, Midwest, and as far as the East Coast. The tour became an annual event.

Sometimes we were paid a small amount of money for the Varsity performances—from one to two hundred dollars a concert. After we paid our expenses, we used the money to make three recordings (one of them in Hollywood), and we sold the records for five dollars each. High schools and conventions regularly used us in their programs. And we even performed with a number of celebrities, including Ed McMahon of the "Tonight Show." The Spring Hill Singers gained recognition throughout the community, and the Varsity became the premiere small ensemble of the deep South.

By then, I had become friends with Thurlow Spurr and felt certain he would support the dream that had unfolded in me when I first heard his group. I gave him a call one night and asked if I might direct one of his groups.

"No," he replied vehemently. "No way, Roger. Going on the road is not all it's cracked up to be. You don't make any money. It'll be hard on your family. You've got a good job at Spring Hill Baptist, and you're serving the Lord. You need to stay where you are."

He went on to tell me of the hardships, the financial strain, and all the other reasons he could think of to explain why I shouldn't go on the road. I listened and I didn't argue. Yet deep in my heart I knew what I wanted to do—and what God wanted me to do.

Linda agreed with Thurlow.

"Honey," she pleaded, "we have two children now." John Roger II was born our last year in Opp, November 1966. Jason Ross was born in May 1970. "We have friends. We're in a wonderful church. Don't you want to be with us?"

"Of course I do, Linda, but this is another opportunity to serve the Lord."

"Roger, it seems to me that you've got more opportunities for service here in Mobile than you can handle right now."

"That may be true, but being tied down to one church is not the kind of ministry for me." I tried to explain what I could do, how important it was for me to train musicians and singers and to minister to churches across the country, not just in Mobile, not just in the South.

My arguments went nowhere. Linda had accepted many other ideas and had been very supportive. But this time her deep fears of my constant traveling—my being gone from home—wouldn't allow her to listen. She was still too dependent on me, and she worried about our two sons growing up without my daily presence. Each time we got this far in the debate, Linda started to cry, and our discussion ended.

Linda and I had never before been in complete disagreement about such a major decision. I understood Linda's feelings. From a logical perspective, both she and Thurlow Spurr made sense. Even so, I couldn't deny what I sensed God calling me to do.

For months I limped along, agonizing over the questions: How *could* I want to go on the road and leave my wife and two sons? How could I leave the choir I had worked so hard to build?

In July 1969 I took Varsity on a ten-day tour, and in

August the Spring Hill Singers and Varsity traveled together. On the road I felt free, totally at peace; I knew I belonged in this field of service for Jesus Christ.

But Linda still wasn't ready to discuss it. "It just doesn't make any sense," she said.

While her reasoning did make sense, I couldn't let go of my dream. "It's just something I want to do," I said, "something I *need* to do." The words sounded weak even to my own ears, but they were true.

For months I went through the agony again and again, and I always came to the same conclusion— going on the road was something I had to do. Each time Varsity made a trip I learned something new. Especially I was learning that God breaks through the normal routines of life and provides the miracles we need through other believers. But He does it in His own time. Financial support for Varsity continued to come in as it was needed, but like Linda, church members thought I was crazy when I talked about going on the road full time. God was teaching me to wait.

Finally, one afternoon during the first week of January 1970, I found myself alone in the church. No phones were ringing and nobody needed to see me. As I sat in the quiet of my office, I decided to write a letter in hopes that it would help me deal with my own inner conflict and help me explain myself more clearly to Linda. I pulled out several sheets of paper, and after staring into space for several minutes, I began to pour out everything I thought and felt. "If I can't even convince my wife that this is the thing I want to do," I wrote, "maybe I'm just crazy. Yet,

Linda, no matter how often I've said those words to myself, the desire won't leave me. I'm miserable. I feel I'm failing you and our sons and everyone else. Right now I'm so confused, I don't know what to do."

Unfortunately, filling up six legal-sized pages didn't lift my spirits this time. No peace, no new ideas came to me. I felt more depressed than when I started.

I never intended for Linda to see the letter—I suppose I was afraid she still wouldn't understand. Instead, I planned to leave the letter at the office and throw it away later. When I got home that evening, however, I saw that I had somehow mixed in the letter with some other papers. I quickly hid it in the back of the middle drawer of my desk, thinking that I would tear it up later. But I didn't tear it up fast enough.

Late one evening when I wasn't home, Linda began to look through my desk for a receipt because a company had billed us a second time. She flipped through a stack of papers and quite accidentally spotted several sheets of yellow ruled paper clipped together. Noticing that the first line on the top page read, "Dear Linda," she curiously picked up the pages, sat down at the desk, and began to read:

I've been trying to explain something to you for weeks now and I know you don't understand. Of all the people in this entire world, you're the one I most need to stand behind me in anything I do. So I'm going to write out what's going on inside me. Maybe by putting it on paper I can say it clearer. . . .

In my letter I never pointed a finger at Linda or accused her of keeping me from God's will. But the more she read, the more she realized the seriousness of this desire of mine: I really felt that God had placed it in my heart. It frightened her to think that she was keeping me from doing what I was sure God wanted me to do, and she cried as she asked for God's forgiveness.

As soon as I came inside the house that night, she ran into my arms.

"Roger, I'm sorry," she choked through her tears, and she hurried to tell me about the letter.

"Oh, Linda," I said, my own eyes brimming with tears. "I never intended for you to see that letter—"

"But God did," she said, "and now I can really be at your side."

As we held one another tightly, I knew the moment I had waited for had arrived. Linda was still afraid, but at least we were standing together now.

God had taught me to wait before sending me out on the road to help carry out Jesus' Great Commission. After a struggle, I seemed about to fulfill my dream of service. But I had no idea of the struggle that lay ahead.

Chapter 2

Moment of Truth

"How does Truth sound?" Linda asked.

"Truth?" I said. "That's a strange kind of name . . . Truth. I like it."

It was very late one evening, months after Linda had agreed that it was God's plan for me to tour with a ministry group. We were sprawled out on our bed with an open Bible before us, searching diligently for just the right name for this new group.

I had been looking for a one-word name. A year earlier a California friend in the recording business had suggested that I drop the word Singers from the name of the youth group I had toured with on weekends. "Just call them Varsity. These days every group has 'singers' tacked on to the end," my friend said. "Think about it. They're everywhere—New World Singers, New Day Singers, New Hope Singers." I had agreed then and had decided to avoid the word in naming our new group. I wanted to sound different, to choose a name that gave us a distinctive identity. Yet it couldn't sound either worldly or preachy.

That night Linda and I had our Bible open because I said, "I'd like a name that comes right from the Bible."

We threw names back and forth and nothing seemed to fit. My first reaction to Truth was to push it aside, too. Yet the more I thought about it, the more I liked it. "Truth it is then," I finally said. We went on to make it an acronym:

T for TRUST
R for RECEIVE
U for UNCHANGEABLE
T for TRUE
H for HAPPINESS IN JESUS

As we repeated the name and uncovered its possibilities, it began to feel just right.

Though it felt just right to us, some others had difficulty with it for a while. When I called pastors or music directors to ask for a booking, they'd ask, "What's the name of the group?"

"TRUTH."

"Truth what?"

"Just TRUTH."

After I explained, they often agreed for us to come. The pastors started announcing to the congregation, "TRUTH is coming." That made for a lot of jokes—"Don't we already have truth in this church?" And some confusion—"Has he been preaching lies all these years?" Thanks to the acronym Linda and I had created, I was able to convince people of our faith and purpose: Trust, Receive, Unchangeable True Happiness in Jesus.

In the first ten years of TRUTH's existence, I learned a lot about how to work with a board of directors. At age twenty-seven I was moving into new areas. Talking with them personally sometimes intimidated me. I knew I would have to learn to be strong concerning my vision for the ministry. Prior to going on the road, I talked regularly with friends in full-time Christian ministry, hoping they might give me insight. Although we can profit from hearing others' stories, we learn some lessons only through experience.

Once things started to happen, I began to recruit singers and musicians. The task before me was monumental. I prayed—hard—asking God to help me find the right instrumentalists and vocalists for TRUTH.

Two leaders and outstanding members in the Varsity joined—Buddy Hornaday and Mike Wells. Buddy, "Mr. Personality," became one of the male singers. He was the featured soloist on our first single for radio air play, "New Life." Along with an appealing innocence and a tremendous willingness to work, Buddy brought a voice with an upbeat, commercial sound to TRUTH. Audiences loved him. Buddy used to get upset with me because I wanted him to sing but would not allow him to drive one of our cars!

Mike Wells joined us to play trombone and to arrange our music. In some ways he was like a son to me. He had grown up without a dad, and sometimes he loved my being a father figure in his life. Sometime he didn't, but more about that later. Whatever the dynamics of our relationship, he is one of the finest musicians ever to be in TRUTH. Their acceptance of my invitation put me well on my way to recruiting just the kind of young people I wanted.

As I continued the selection process and after we were on the road, these two young men, who had worked with me for several years, knew my working style and were a great asset to me.

Vince Harris came to TRUTH as a trombonist, and Ricky Spears signed on to play trumpet. They were both outstanding high school musicians, and they were best friends. Another Mobile boy, Jerome Gilmer, became TRUTH's first keyboard player. He was nothing short of a young genius. Jerome didn't stay with us long enough, but he certainly contributed mightily to our getting off to a good start.

Donna Taylor, talented and sweet, became our second soprano. Her dad was a minister of music too, and we were friends. Beyond her own talent Donna brought the knowledge and commitment that come from being reared in a musical family.

Then a source at Samford University in Birmingham gave an excellent recommendation for an alto named Marty Feazell, a pastor's daughter. She was vivacious and outgoing, tall and blond. After I heard her sing, I knew I wanted her with TRUTH. But there was a problem. Marty had a boyfriend named Joe Estes, and she didn't want to travel a year without him.

Now Joe was a good tenor and a great musician. His trumpet and guitar playing were "too good to be true." He also played bass. But he was making good money in a successful bluegrass band. Joe had grown up in the church but was nowhere near being a committed Christian. Yet he seemed to be exactly what I wanted musically. When I invited Joe to join TRUTH, he didn't laugh at me, but he said, "There's no way I'd be interested in going along with a group like TRUTH."

"Would you think about it?" I said.

"Oh, I'll think about it," he said, but his words indicated he wouldn't think about it very much. I felt led to stay in contact with Joe, and about a month later, when I invited him again, he said, "Okay, Mr. Breland, I'll go with you for a year."

Then Joe recommended a friend from Samford, Steve Burks, to play bass guitar. Steve became our funny man, always the life of the party. He kept us laughing with his practical jokes and crazy sense of humor. One night when we were on the road and I was introducing TRUTH, I couldn't find him. He had slipped off the stage and I found him in the balcony.

TRUTH's first drummer, Mark Hardy, had just gotten out of the army and showed up on my doorstep. He had quite a past. Although raised by godly parents in Paris, Texas, he had gotten into drugs in his service in Vietnam and had gone AWOL a few times. Then Mark met Jesus Christ. "I'm hungry for spiritual things," he said. "I want to serve the Lord." The day he showed up at my front door, he asked if he would have to wear a choir robe to play his drums. I believe he would have been willing to! Mark, a nice looking, dark-haired young man with a mustache, was a great blues-type singer as well as drummer—the only TRUTH drummer who ever sang from the drums. Audience response was tremendous whenever Mark sang "I Don't Know Why Jesus Loved Me" or "Put Your Hand in the Hand" as he played the drums.

Mark also communicated well with people, especially street people. He had been saved out of the drug culture and had a real message to share with them. He became a spiritual leader with TRUTH and ministered to thousands our first year.

Our marvelous first soprano came to us from Campus Crusade staff at the University of Missouri. She was a beautiful young woman named Jan Stevens. Her experiences with Campus Crusade made her a great help to the other TRUTH members, who were learning how to share their testimonies.

Handsome Fred Sharrett came to us from Tennessee. What a great singer! Later in the year Fred's twin brother Ed joined TRUTH as well. These two were really a blessing. They were very close, and they were both young preachers. The girls usually surrounded these two!

Right at the start I leveled with these young people about finances: "If you're invited to become a member of TRUTH, you're starting on a venture of faith with little money." They had to pay for their own transportation to get to me for an audition and their way home afterward.

Those who joined TRUTH had to understand that they weren't going to make a fortune. Actually, they weren't really going to make any money. "You'll receive fifteen dollars a week," I said before I invited them to join us. "TRUTH will pay all your normal expenses, like food and lodging."

When we left on tour in June of 1971, I had fifteen members. We were all young; several members had just graduated from high school. Even I was young. For three years I taught high school, and I had learned a lot by common sense and practical experience. Yet God had so much to teach me. I asked each member to stay for one year. When I formed TRUTH, I planned to begin with fresh talent each year. In the twenty-year life of TRUTH, we've made many changes, but that's how we started.

In fact, we had to begin making changes in the first year. When Jerome left, Kathy Taylor from Mobile College came to help us at the keyboard. She was a talented music teacher and a church pianist. She played keyboard until April, when we recruited the energetic, exciting Mr. Gordon Twist. Gordon was a graduate of a Christian college and one of the most gifted musicians I'd ever met. He not only played keyboard, but he sang, wrote, directed, arranged, and did all of them well. Gordon is truly a musician's musician. Kathy stayed with us as a singer. Bill Farnum was our second sound engineer. I was the first. You can imagine how excited we were to have him join in the fall of 1971.

Gary Hannie, another of my guys from the Spring Hill days, joined later in the year to play trumpet. Gary did a good job. And he had a personal trait that was awfully useful on the road; he was "Mr. Together" with everything organized from briefcase to suitcase.

A heavy blow fell when Marty Feazell developed serious vocal problems and needed total vocal rest. But God provided us with a replacement, Fern Strait, a sweet little girl with a big voice. She joined us from Hardin-Simmons University.

As we moved through TRUTH's first year, I continued to pray for and with these wonderful, dedicated young men and women. It would have been impossible to do what we did for even a week without their intense commitment. Nowadays when I interview and audition prospective members, I tell them, "I consider three categories: your head, your heart, and your talent. And you have to have all three." My first group on the road taught me much about the immense value of these three qualities.

I also learned to respect the right of the members' individual identity. In 1972, our second year, that respect was put to the test. We had an invitation to sing in Springfield, Missouri—the double Vatican where both the Assemblies of God and the Bible Baptists have their headquarters. One of the larger Bible Baptist churches had invited us. We arrived on Wednesday afternoon, and the janitor who let us in treated everyone a little rudely. Even so, we immediately set up our equipment. Our kids practiced a few of their songs. Two hours later, the pastor walked in, greeted me, and then said, "Roger, we have a problem."

As we walked outside the room I said, "Pastor, if you're concerned about the volume, don't worry about it. You won't have a problem. We'll keep it down."

"No, not the sound."

Naturally confused, I asked, "What *is* the problem?"

"Your hair is too long."

Most of the guys wore their hair a bit long, but it

was well groomed. They looked nothing like the rock-and-rollers. By then the janitor had come up and stood next to the pastor. He had obviously been listening because he said, "Yeah, it's so long that if it had been my decision, I would not have even allowed you to come inside and unload. I would have mentioned it to you as soon as you came in." I could hardly believe what they were saying, and I must have shown my shock.

"The solution," said the pastor, "is simple. All you have to do is take your boys and go out and get haircuts so you can sing tonight."

"You honestly mean that?" I tried to think of what to say. I glanced at my watch: four-thirty. We still had to eat dinner, change clothes, and meet for our prayer time prior to the concert.

"If you don't," he said, "you can't sing tonight."

"Give me a little time to talk to the others," I said. Back inside, I called all the members of TRUTH to sit down in the front row. I told them the situation. "What are you going to do?" asked Mark.

By then, I knew what to do. I told them. Then I went out into the hallway and said to the pastor, "We'll just leave. Rushing everyone to the barber shop is just a little too much to ask." We loaded our equipment and checked into the closest, least expensive motel. The kids appreciated my stand, but they were feeling low. It might have been a low moment for me, but I tried not to let it get me down. "There's more than one Baptist church in town," I said half-aloud to myself.

Once I was checked into my room, I pulled out the yellow pages of the Springfield telephone directory. I called the First Baptist Church, and to my surprise I was able to speak with the senior minister, Dr. T. T. Crabtree. "Pastor," I said, "my name is Roger Breland. I'm a former minister of music in Baptist churches. I don't know you, and you don't know anything about me. However, I thought you might know the church I came from." He knew my home church and many of the people there.

Once I had established that I wasn't just some fellow off the street, I told him the story of what had happened at the other church. "This has really devastated my people. I wanted to know if you would consider letting us come to your church to sing just one song? We don't need a meal or an offering. We're not asking for anything, but this experience is so affecting the members of my group that I don't know what's going to happen."

"You sure can come."

God used this good man to minister to TRUTH.

Once we set up at First Church, Dr. Crabtree said, "We'd like you to do more than one song." He actually let us sing for thirty minutes. And that wasn't all. After we finished, Dr. Crabtree said, "We want to give these wonderful young people a love offering." The church even took all of us out for a steak dinner afterward! In the early years, we went back to First Church several times. We always had great response. Even today, when I walk into the building, I remember 1972 when we had no place to go and they took us in.

Strangely and sadly, the other church no longer exists. Within months, the church membership began to decline, and they finally closed their doors.

~

That first year the plan was to work from July through May, take a couple of weeks off, begin rehearsals in June, and be on the road again by the first of July with the new members. During our first few seasons, I invited two or three people to stay on, but basically it was a new group every year. As I would later realize, breaking in a virtually new group each year only increased the difficulty.

And there were difficulties. When we began, one of the desperate needs was for transportation. Since we didn't have the money to buy, we leased three station wagons and purchased one truck to haul the equipment. We also had to find a place to rehearse, homes to stay in, and sound equipment. With hard work and the help of a board of directors, we met these needs and found ourselves actually ready to go on the road. The waiting was over (or so I thought), and the ministry was begun.

My verse for TRUTH became 1 Thessalonians 2:4: "But as we have been approved by God to be entrusted with the gospel, even so we speak, not as pleasing men, but God who tests our hearts." As I struggled with trying to please men, God always seemed to bring me back to the words in this verse. Just to please Him became the desire and drive of my life.

Oh! Was it ever hard to wave good-bye to my family and begin this journey! But deep in my heart I felt the peace of being right where God wanted me—in the center of His will.

Chapter 3

A Lonely Moment

I was a little too optimistic. In fact, I was downright gullible. No one could have prepared me for life on the road.

For two months in the summer of 1971, I had auditioned and trained a group of fifteen to go on the road. We had what we referred to as our first rehearsal camp at a local college in Mobile. About the time we started our rehearsal, Bill Buchanan handed me a check for $2,500. Bill was my dear friend who believed in me and supported me. For the rehearsal time and our first three months on the road, that money would be our financial backing.

I was about to venture out on a dream. This traveling music ministry was the beginning of a new way of life for my family. It would be an adjustment for all of us. But I was out to prove that I could do it.

That first year I didn't prove much except that going on the road was very difficult.

The night before we left on our tour, in June 1971, an optometrist and friend, Dr. Win Ritchie, visited us at our orientation camp to give us a devotional message. I was ready to listen because I trusted him. He and his wife Nell have proven themselves many times to be faithful friends.

Among the things Dr. Ritchie said, I particularly remember these words: "You're going to be coming into contact with a lot of people out there. Some of them are going to like what you do. They'll like you regardless of how badly you sing. But no matter how hard you work, all of them won't like you. Some of them won't like you despite what you accomplish."

In the same message he said, "If you don't spend time with God privately, he won't use you publicly."

I've since put that comment into my own words: "God will never use you publicly until he tutors you privately." Dr. Ritchie's words hit me pretty hard and forced me to look at myself more closely.

I was so involved in the life of the church, but I didn't always have time for God. I was doing religious things, good things: speaking, teaching, going to rehearsals. I was very, very busy for God—too busy. It wasn't that I didn't read the Bible or pray, but I didn't daily set aside quality time. I didn't change immediately after his message to us. Not until I started traveling on the road did I develop devotional habits and the discipline to give God quality time in my life.

I wish I could say it was because a light turned on and I cried, "Yes, Lord."

The truth is less exciting.

Traveling can be boring and lonely. Out of loneliness and longing for my wife and sons, I turned to God in a deeper way than ever before.

Just before Dr. Ritchie paused to pray for us, he looked squarely at me and said, "Roger, this part is for you. There's a verse I want to give you from 1 Thessalonians." He paused for me to open my Bible. "It's 1 Thessalonians 2:4: 'But as we have been approved by God to be entrusted with the gospel, even so we speak, not as pleasing men, but God who tests our hearts.'"

Through all of these years, that verse has stayed with me as the theme verse of TRUTH. When I've faced discouragements—and I've had my share of them—these words from Paul have often helped me.

We were ready to go to our first concert. I said the painful good-bye to my family, and we drove straight from Mobile to Florence, Alabama. The trip took us nine hours. If I had known what lay ahead, I might never have started out.

When we got there, we realized that they hadn't scheduled us to perform at the church. The minister of music had arranged for us to sing outside at a small picnic area. That was fine with us. We figured people on the highway could hear us and just might pull in to listen. We rushed to set up our equipment and could hardly wait to sing. Several times I looked skyward and noticed heavy rain clouds crawling toward us. I didn't worry—I just knew that God would hold off the rain until we had done our first big concert. By the time we had everything set up, it was five-thirty. "I'm going to rush over and register at the motel and get cleaned up a little," I said.

All the way to the motel, my mind was churning. It

was our first concert, and I wanted it to be wonderful. The clouds had darkened, and I kept praying, *Oh, God, don't let the rain come until we finish the concert*. When I pulled up at the motel, I set my two suitcases down behind the car and went inside to register. When I came out, instead of going forward, I only needed to back up about fifty feet. As I backed up, I heard a terrible sound as if my muffler were being torn off. "Oh, no!" Too late I remembered my suitcases. When I resigned as minister of music there, the members of Spring Hill Baptist Church had given me that beautiful black, three-piece set of luggage as a going-away present: a briefcase, a suitcase, and a carry-on. They were the nicest cases I'd ever owned.

I cut the engine and hurried around to look at my luggage.

Too late!

The suitcases couldn't have looked worse if I had planned to demolish them.

Reminding myself that they were only suitcases— even though I had already become attached to them—I hurried on to the concert. It was a hot, muggy summer day in Florence, and the sky continued to darken. The crowd was smaller than we had expected. While we were doing our opening song, I felt a few sprinkles, but we kept on. Just as we were finishing our second number, the clouds of heaven opened up. In twelve seconds we had no audience, and everyone on the platform was running for cover. The girls' new clothes were drenched. We received no offering, of course. Our spirits were dampened along with our bodies.

When I called Linda that night, I was really down. I don't remember what she said, but just having an understanding and caring wife at home did make me feel better. That was the first of many calls that encouraged me through the years on the road.

"Oh, well," I said to the group, "no one can say we didn't have a poor beginning." I was determined not to get discouraged. This was, after all, only our first concert.

The people in Florence provided sleeping quarters for the members of TRUTH. I went to the motel where I could be alone, pray, think, and make a few phone calls to set up concerts. *My first day on the road,* I thought, *and everything is ruined. Is this the way my ministry is going to go?*

By morning my spirits had picked up, and we drove the truck and the leased cars from Florence to the little town of Iuka in northern Mississippi. My friend Jerry Swimmer, a great musician and former minister of music in Mobile who is now in full-time evangelism had moved to Iuka. When I called Jerry and told him about my vision for TRUTH, I added, "We need a place to start, to show people what we do."

"Then come on to Iuka!"

Exactly what I had expected from Jerry.

As I started to thank him, he said, "You have to understand, this isn't First Baptist, Roger, but it's the biggest Baptist church in town." Then he laughed, "Oh, and besides that, it's the only Baptist church."

After my call to Jerry Swimmer and reflecting on my previous experience of booking concerts with my other groups, I said to Linda, "Look, I could book this thing for six months straight just because of my friends."

I soon learned how naive I was. In fact, many of those friends would be the last to book us—if at all. Many of them weren't willing to take a chance on us. One pastor, who I had assumed was a good friend and whom I just knew I could count on, said something like, "You got a good heart, Roger, but I just don't know if your group is going to make it. I'll wait and see if you can make it on the road."

We didn't exactly die on the road. We gasped for breath several times, but we always managed to survive.

We spent a week in and around Iuka, a nice little town that has one traffic signal. We learned right then that the smallness of the town or the church doesn't mean anything.

A few months after we began touring, I thought that a full-time booking agent would make everything easier for us, and I called a musician named Johnny Speedling. Johnny had been a friend of mine since high school days and a member of a quartet I once sang in. He's a happy, friendly person who loves people and is an excellent soloist.

Because he believed in TRUTH, Johnny resigned from his position as minister of music and became our full-time booking agent. Across the Southeast and Midwest he traveled from church to church, trying to book us. He had a lonely, difficult job. Johnny held on for six months—longer than he should have in such a rough job. He gave it everything he had.

Shortly afterward he went back to a church position. That left the burden on me. Once again I resorted to the telephone because I had to travel with TRUTH. Again I became the booking agent, making arrangements for future concerts while we were on the road. It was a harried and frustrating experience, but it was the best we could do.

When we reached a church, the group set up while I talked to the preacher about the concert that night. If we didn't have a place to go the next day I'd ask, "Can you think of something we can do tomorrow? We want to sing for the Lord. Anything. The local high school. The Ladies' Missionary Union. Do you have a pastor-friend I can call?" I assumed that every pastor has at least five pastor friends.

Most of them called their friends quite willingly because people want to help. Each time a pastor did that, it meant one more contact for TRUTH. We also tried to offer them a good musical program with an emphasis upon the love of God. We assumed that if we gave it our best, we could return in the future. In a few instances, instead of waiting a year or more, I'd try to go back in three to six months just so we could keep busy.

We did a lot of revivals too. Churches all over the country were holding summer and fall revivals, and when I heard about one, I contacted the pastor: "Let us do twenty minutes of special music." Many of them agreed. They usually put us up overnight and gave us a hundred dollars. That wasn't a lot of money, but we were making contacts and building for the future. And they always allowed us to sell our records. I did my best just to get us in front of people. And once they heard us, I just knew they'd want to hear us again. And most of the time, we did get invited back.

Whenever TRUTH sang, I announced, "If you'd like to become part of this group, talk to me later and we'll set up an audition." Through the years I took that approach and discovered a lot of extraordinary talent. Now that TRUTH is firmly established, most prospective singers and musicians contact us.

In our first forty-nine weeks on the road, we did 374 concerts with almost no days off. My goal was for us to sing somewhere every day. Many times we did two or three concerts a day—a junior high school or high school during the day and then a concert that night. We averaged eight concerts a week.

In the years ahead, we would learn that some of our most wonderful experiences occurred when we had small gatherings. The old joke I tell about the beginning of our ministry goes, "In the beginning, we were so poor we were playing for grand openings of service stations, back-yard barbecues, and missionary luncheons." That's pretty close to what we did! One time we set up in front of Woolworth at a mall in Lexington, Kentucky. We didn't have any other place to perform.

The manager of Woolworth was a Christian, and he must have felt sorry for us. He even fed us lunch.

Believe it or not, I booked several concerts in churches by playing the Turfland Mall in Lexington. A local pastor, who was walking along, paused to listen and then asked me who we were. He ended up inviting us to sing at his church. A Lexington family kept all of us in their home one night.

Several times that summer we set up in public

places because at that point we were more concerned about just having a place to sing than we were in making money. It's a good thing too; we sure didn't make any money. Our biggest offering was $310. A typical offering was $65.

Before a concert in a small, country church, one of our sopranos discovered that the only restroom was outdoors. She returned to the prayer room, red-faced. We all laughed. Yet we were to learn that this was only the first of such places. And we learned to accept whatever conditions the people offered us. I asked for one more thing: a hotel room where I could have a few hours away from TRUTH and everyone else. Almost every time the people at the sponsoring church understood and provided this accommodation.

We had our hard times, but the moments of blessing came as well. George Dooms, the head of the local Youth for Christ, opened doors for us in Evansville, Indiana. One night in Rome, Georgia, at a football stadium, we gave an invitation for people to turn their lives over to Jesus Christ. We watched in joyful amazement as 250 people came forward.

Our concerts always included personal testimonies. Our drummer-singer, Mark Hardy, often told how he met Jesus Christ. No matter how many times I heard him, it was thrilling to listen to him. I'll probably never forget the high school assembly at Fort Myers, Florida. Mark shared about his drug use and about a godly father who prayed for him every day. Then he stopped right in the middle of what he was saying and pointed to a couple of kids in the audience. "You guys! I can look at you right now and tell that you're on drugs. And you need to stop it right now, or drugs will ruin your life." Then he told the rest of his story. His sincerity commanded attention. He had the look of a musician, knew about all their rock and roll jargon, and was totally believable.

Mark ministered to a lot of people that first year, musically as well as with his testimony. One four-year-old boy went crazy over Mark's playing. Mark took the boy to church, set up his drums, and let the kid play them as long as he wanted. Without even realizing it, Mark challenged me in my own spiritual growth. He had a copy of the Living Bible and would sit in the back seat of our station wagon and read. Sometimes he'd burst out laughing and say, "I can't believe this! It's too fantastic!" He meant that, as he read the Bible, he just couldn't get over how wonderful the Scriptures were. They were alive to him.

~

During those first weeks on the road, I was as homesick as any of the others. Linda was home changing diapers, caring for John and Jason, expecting our third son, Jeremy, and teaching school. I missed her and them.

When I kissed her good-bye, I planned to be gone for six weeks. That's the longest I had ever been away (and I've never been away that long since then). I was out to prove that I could do it. That first year I didn't prove much except that Thurlow Spurr was right—going on the road was *hard*.

Linda wasn't having a particularly easy time of it

either. She was responsible for developing and maintaining a totally new way of life for my family. Her task was to stay home and raise our sons.

I must say she did a wonderful job of nurturing our boys while I was on the road. She has said that however difficult her days might become, she always found prayer to be a great help. Through prayer and her Bible she learned to love each boy and accept him the way he was. She always chose to honor God, to love Him, to read her Bible, to pray, and to reach out to help others. Our boys couldn't have had a better model for their lives than a godly mother. Several verses were real sources of strength to Linda during those early days of TRUTH:

"Whenever I am afraid,
I will trust in You."
   Psalm 56:3

"From the end of the earth I will cry to You,
When my heart is overwhelmed;
Lead me to the rock that is higher than I."
   Psalm 61:2

One word of wisdom she passes along from this experience is: Some of my worst days have been some of my greatest days spiritually. She found God faithful to His promise of Jeremiah 29:13: "And you will seek Me and find Me, when you search for Me with all your heart." So did I!

From the first day I began traveling, I wrote or called them daily. On June 29, 1971, I wrote my first letter to Linda and the boys. That one-page letter was crammed full of my love and my longing to be with them.

Dear John and Jason,
I really miss you! Sorry you were asleep this morning when I
left. Dad loves you very much, and while I'm away there are
some things I want both of you to do!

John:
(1) Do exactly what Mom says.
(2) Do not go to the pool alone.
(3) Clean up your toys.
(4) Be sweet to Jason.
(5) Help Mommy!

Jason:
(1) Stay off the stairs.
(2) Do not bother the new stereo.
(3) Sleep all night.
(4) Stay out of the cabinets.

Daddy loves you both very much.

I wanted my letter to assure Linda and the boys of
my love and concern. I concluded:

Linda, I really hated to leave this morning. When I kissed
John and Jason, I almost cried. I just know the next one will
be just like them. I'm really excited about the new addition.
Take good care of yourself and go to the doctor this week.

Five months later, in late November when Linda
was eight months pregnant, she received a letter
from me that she says she especially prizes. The un-
dertones spoke of my missing my family and my
feeling lonely, but at the same time I wrote of my un-
swerving certainty that I was doing what God had
called me to do. Part of it reads:

Couldn't sleep so I wanted to write you this note. Sure felt
bad after I talked to you tonight. I know you are having a

rough time with the boys, and I'm sure you feel terrible these days. Wish I were there to help you.

God knows I think about you all the time. Linda, there's not much I can really say about what's happening in our lives right now. It's all so fast and new until I can hardly believe it has all taken place. But there's one thing you must never forget—that is, I love you very much.

Thank you for being understanding and taking care of my boys! It takes a special kind of girl to love and put up with a guy like me. And I thank you for being extra special.

I feel a real sense of God's will consistently as we travel. He is really dealing with me right now, and I want you to pray for me. Honey, God's got something he wants me to do, and I'm completely open to his will. I've never really hungered for spiritual things, but I find myself daily talking with God about this ministry.

I'm terribly excited about the future! I know this ministry is difficult for you—no husband or dad. But I'm confident that the future is bright. Let's just hang on for a while and give God a chance to really work!

Jeremy Ryan, our third son, a special gift from the Lord, was born in December 1971. We gave a concert in Mobile the night before. Very early the morning of the 30th we went to the hospital.

TRUTH seldom knew more than a day or two ahead of time where we'd sing. I learned to cope with that. Finances were a constant problem before us, and I learned to live with that.

I missed my family a lot, and I'm not sure I fully learned how not to feel lonely. Writing and phoning helped, but I missed them every day I was on the road. As crazy as it may sound, I left home to travel with TRUTH, but I really never left home. My heart was always there. I communicated with Linda about every little detail. She was very much a part of my life and ministry on the road. I had to struggle to hold my focus on the goals of the ministry, to learn to be alone with God. During TRUTH's early years I often found comfort in repeating the verse that Dr. Ritchie gave me before we started out: "But as we have been approved by God to be entrusted with the gospel, even so we speak, not as pleasing men, but God who tests our hearts."

Especially, I thought, *God who tests our hearts. But, Lord, will it always have to be so hard?*

Chapter 4

A Musical Moment

Ups and downs. Joys and heartaches. I went out on the road with TRUTH, naive but doing the best I knew how. I discovered that even though the first weeks and months were so difficult, it didn't always have to be so hard. In fact, I often think of our first five or six years on the road as the glory years. We didn't always see the glory at the time, but all across the country people were learning to accept us and our music.

We were definitely on the cutting edge as we introduced contemporary Christian music to local congregations. My friend, Bill Gaither, said to me once, "Roger, when I look South, I bow twice—once to Ronn Huff and once to you—for introducing my music south of the Mason-Dixon line."

So many things happened during those first five or six years. And most of them led directly or indirectly to spiritual and musical growth. In the early days I tried a number of different things because it was my first attempt to direct and manage a touring group on a full-time basis.

~

I did know that we needed to get out a record to help us build a reputation. Before we went on the road, TRUTH cut a custom record. Once we had the albums, we set up a table at each concert and sold our records for five dollars each. Often we made more money from the records than we received in the night's offerings. In the years that followed, when we returned to places, I was repeatedly amazed when people told me how much they liked the record and that they still played it regularly. Since those who bought the records told their friends, it wasn't unusual to get invited to a church because the choir director or someone had heard the record and liked our sound.

In the fall of 1971 I flew to Kansas City to see the premiere of the Spurrlows' new gospel multimedia musical called *Love*. I liked staying abreast of contemporary music. I had also hosted Spurr and the Spurrlows many times when I was a minister of music, and continued to appreciate them and their influence.

When I arrived at the airport, I looked around, not sure what to do next. My immediate thought was to catch a ride to the auditorium. I didn't know about renting a car, and I wouldn't have had the money had I known. I ran into one minister I knew, and he introduced me to Wayne Buchanan. "Since we're both going to the same place," I said to Wayne, "would you mind giving me a ride?" "Not at all," he said. "I'd be glad to give you a lift."

As we drove into the city, I asked, "What kind of work do you do?"

"I'm the sales manager for the Benson Company in Nashville."

"The record people?"

"That's right."

The Benson Company was making quite a name for itself putting out solid contemporary Christian music—producing records for the Gaithers, Doug Oldham, and the Imperials, among others. Wayne was in charge of the multimedia part of the musical. Finally he asked, "Roger, what kind of work do you do?" I told him everything anyone could ever want to know about TRUTH. Then he spoke the most beautiful words in the world: "I'd like to hear the group sometime."

"Would you really? I'd love for you to attend a concert."

"Let me know your schedule, and I'll see what I can do about getting to one of your concerts."

That was all I needed to hear. I gave him our itinerary for the next month.

Love was superbly done, and the crowd responded enthusiastically. As I left that night after the musical, I felt like a failure. We sounded pretty dismal by comparison with the best group in the business. I forgot that TRUTH had been together only a few months and the Spurrlows had sung together for years. I suppose because of my own insecurity, I looked to someone else and wanted TRUTH to be like them instead of being who we were. I had yet to learn that being who we were was enough.

When I returned, I called the members of TRUTH together. "We've got to work harder; we've got to improve musically. If we give God our all, I know we can do a better job."

Two weeks later, when we were at Huntsville, Alabama, Wayne Buchanan and his wife, Sue, drove down just to see us. "You've got a good group," Wayne said afterward. "I'm impressed."

I wasn't sure what impressed meant. It could have been a polite way of getting out of there or it could have meant that he liked us. "Let me tell you how it works, Roger," Wayne said. "I'm going back to Nashville and talk to Bob MacKenzie about TRUTH. If I can convince him you're worth hearing, he'll come to one of your concerts."

That was encouraging news. Bob MacKenzie's visit could mean a connection to one of the best Christian music companies in the world. However, when I didn't hear anything for a couple of weeks, I figured that was the end of the matter.

Then Wayne called me. "Bob MacKenzie is going to fly down to Jackson, Mississippi, to your concert next week. If he's interested, he'll want to talk further."

Wayne was referring to our invitation to sing for two days at a youth convention in December 1971. Fifteen hundred youth and youth leaders attended. The exposure at the convention opened many doors for us, including a return engagement the following year. We sang more concerts in Mississippi in 1972 than in any other state. "If there had not been a Mississippi," I've said often, "there wouldn't be a TRUTH today."

Bob MacKenzie did come to the concert. He's about five-feet-eight with brown hair and was in his thirties. The minute we met, I liked the man. Even today I think of him as a bundle of energy and brilliance—a creative genius. And the insights he shared with me that night have helped TRUTH all the way through to today.

After the concert I sat with Bob in a hotel room, and we talked about TRUTH, about gospel music, about the future of musical groups. He liked us and I was stunned. Again, I was comparing us to the Spurrlows and other groups and seeing us as inferior.

"I like TRUTH," Bob said, "because you don't sing head music, but heart music." He didn't know it, but he was handing me valuable insights. Although I had intuitively selected music that aimed for the heart of the audience, from then on, I did it more consciously.

Then Bob MacKenzie taught me something else I've never forgotten. "You need to sing to the guy on the third row. Does the guy on the third row like what's happening?"

I shrugged. "I don't know. Who is he?"

"Let's look at him," Bob said. "First, he didn't want to come. He probably has a little grease under his fingernails, and his wife or kids made him come. He doesn't like your kind of music, so he's sitting there with his arms folded, saying, 'Bless me—I dare you.' If you bless him, he'll be blessed. Now, does the guy on the third row like what's going on?"

"I need to find a way to get him to listen, don't I?"

"Roger, if you can communicate with that man in the third row, the rest of the people will eavesdrop and hear what you're saying to him. If you break through to him, you'll break through to most of the people there." For the first time I understood, and it was what I needed to hear. Bob wanted me to think of the audience as individuals, to communicate in such a compelling, personal way that they would want to listen. Since that conversation, I regularly say to TRUTH, "Let's just talk to the guy in the third row. Make it that personal. And let everybody else listen. If you try to speak to the crowds, you become too impersonal. Concentrate on one or two people."

In a matter of hours, Bob MacKenzie taught me a lot by pushing me to look at music and concerts from the perspective of the audience. No matter what happened after that, I knew I'd always be thankful to him.

"What do you think about making albums?" he asked. He suggested that TRUTH might record with Benson.

"I've got mixed feelings about it," I said. Then I told him where I stood. "I think it's pretty commercial and not very spiritual." I spoke out of my preconceived ideas about the people who traveled full time and recorded. Many of those I knew personally or knew about were pretty slick and not very believable. It didn't seem necessary to air my criticism though, so all I said was, "I'm not sure it's a good idea to record an album. I don't want to be lumped into the category of a lot of what's out there today."

"Oh, I know about some of them too. And a lot of the stories are true," he said. "I also know stories about preachers. Even a few tales about dishonest deacons too. But you know, Roger, I still go to church and I still listen to preaching."

"Guess I hadn't thought of it that way," I said. Unwilling to give up so quickly, I told him, "I've got one record we put together ourselves. It's sold pretty well. But, frankly, this professional record-making sounds pretty commercial to me."

"That's true—or at least partly true. The Benson Company has to make a profit to stay in business. But we also offer a service to God's people. We try to present quality music they can play in their homes. As you probably know, sometimes a song reaches a person who wouldn't listen to a sermon."

For nearly an hour, Bob talked about the vision behind the Benson Company. Most of all, he really conveyed to me that it was an opportunity to minister. Finally he said, "Roger, I'd like you to sign a contract for TRUTH to record with us." I was ready to sign— no more arguments and no reservations.

I signed a three-year contract in January 1972.

Since then, TRUTH has made over forty albums, most of them with Benson. Bob MacKenzie's offer provided one of our first big breaks by giving us wider exposure. The records provided us national credibility that we wouldn't ordinarily have had. Our records never became Benson's top seller, but we had good, consistent sales and, over the years, built up a loyal following.

A short time after we started recording for Benson, MacKenzie arranged for us to use Bill Gaither's studio in Alexandria, Indiana, for six days. Obviously he knew what he was doing. We recorded two albums at one time. And it was work! We started by nine in the morning and stayed until midnight. The group called Re Generation came in at midnight and worked till eight the next morning. By the end of the week Bob had produced three records. It was bizarre, but that's the way he did it in the old days.

In the ensuing dozen years, Bob MacKenzie would have a major creative and spiritual impact on my life. I consider Bob my musical mentor and a special friend. He took me under his wing and guided me, helping me to understand the music business.

Our first album called *Truth* came out in the spring of 1972. It featured "My Tribute" and "New Life." We thought it was the greatest recording in the world! Even today, when I hear it, I think it's good.

In 1972, a college freshman named Steve Taylor wanted to become a member of TRUTH. I liked Steve—he's one of those individuals who is just fun to be around. I had known him since he was in high school in Greenville, South Carolina. His dad is an outstanding music evangelist. But I felt Steve needed to become a stronger vocalist before coming to TRUTH.

"Tell you what," I said, "go on back to college. Get a little more experience. After that, if you're still interested, let's talk." I had no way of knowing that I would see Steve again or that he would have an ongoing relationship with us.

I did hire Steve's friend, Russell, as our drummer after Mark Hardy left. About a week before coming to our rehearsal camp, Russell phoned me. "I just don't think I can come. My folks don't really want me to, none of my friends think I ought to do it, and my girlfriend doesn't want me to leave." Immediately panic set in because I had filled all the places, and everything was set. I calmed myself down and said, "Russell, you've talked to a lot of people, but have you talked to God about it?"

"No, not really," he said.

"Why don't you talk to the Lord about this decision? Call me back. We're expecting you here in a few days, and it'll be a real blow to us if you can't make it." I didn't know it at the time, but this would often be the response from people I auditioned. It was a lonely decision to join TRUTH because they would come without encouragement.

"I was desperate to know what to do," Russell said when he called back the next day. "I prayed for God to show me. Then I opened up the Living Bible and the first thing I read was Galatians 5:7."

Here's the verse he read: "You were getting along so well. Who has interfered with you to hold you back from following the truth?" (TLB) Russell continued, "When I read 'the truth' I knew God meant TRUTH. I just want you to know that I'll be there."

Off and on during our year together, Russell spoke about Steve. They had grown up together and had sung in the same ensemble in church. About then Joe Estes left us for a short time, and I called Steve to fill in. He did a good job, but I still didn't think it was his time yet. He returned to school and finished his degree. About a year or so after college, Steve came to be with TRUTH full time. He is so talented, and he ultimately wanted to be a record producer.

When Steve left TRUTH, we sent him to Nashville to represent TRUTH. He looked for new songs for us and has gone on to do well in Christian recording. Now known as Steven V. Taylor, he has become one of the top producers in Christian music. I am very proud of him.

In 1973 I hired a young man from Louisville, Kentucky, named Greg Golden, to run sound for us. He was quiet, highly intelligent, and very dedicated. After watching Greg on the road and noticing how warmly and efficiently he worked with the other members of TRUTH, I said to him, "Greg, I'd like you to come back. . . ." He beamed. "But not on the road. I need some capable person in the office, someone who can talk to people. It's mainly to do our bookings."

After I explained the other parts of the job, Greg agreed to work in the office "for a while." After eighteen years, he's still with us. I have no idea how TRUTH would function without him.

We finally got out of the station wagon business in 1972 by purchasing a used bus. In 1973 we traded that in on a second one, a 1961 Silver Eagle. It looked great—but it was quite a task to keep it running.

Bus troubles never seemed to leave us very long. Finally, in July 1974, I borrowed $99,000 to buy TRUTH's first new bus. Despite the high interest rates and soaring fuel prices that winter, we were able to pay it off eighteen months early.

~

In 1973 we tried doing civic club luncheons at noon. We received no honorarium, only free lunches and a chance to sell our records. For these groups we sang a patriotic package and announced our evening church concert. That did help our finances, but it was too hard on us because it called for twelve concerts a week.

In 1974 we made our first live album in Clarksdale, Mississippi: *You Don't Know What You're Missin'*. The members of TRUTH really gave their best, and the album was nominated for a Grammy award. In June we sang at the Southern Baptist Convention for the Evangelists' Conference in Dallas. When we sang "The Church Triumphant," the audience stood and cheered us. A memorable experience for us.

In 1975 we sang again at the Southern Baptist Convention in Miami. Among other high moments, we personally met a number of the prominent leaders of the convention. Bill Gaither invited us to Indianapolis, Indiana, to participate in the first Praise Gathering of Believers, which featured Corrie Ten Boom. This was doubly exciting because TRUTH was still relatively unknown. We sang "The Church Triumphant," and the audience response was tremendous. After the concert, we had the greatest record sale in our history.

The following year we did another Praise Gathering of Believers at Indianapolis—seven thousand people. I didn't feel that we contributed to the program the way I had hoped. But that, I've had to realize, is also part of the growing process.

The times when the reception was less warm were hard on the kids too. I'll always be grateful for the loyalty they showed. They sacrificed and postponed their career plans to do what God called them to do— to be a part of TRUTH.

One night, two years after the signing of our first contract with the Benson Recording Company, Bob MacKenzie said, "Roger, you have this group. They're talented and they perform well."

Before I had a chance to absorb the compliment and respond, Bob asked, "But what are you trying to say with this group?"

"Say?" I was stunned by his asking. "I'm not trying to say anything. We just want to share our music."

"Think about it some more." Until then I had thought I needed only to collect a group of talented kids, dress them well, train them to sing the right notes with a little style—and everybody would like TRUTH.

"But what's your focus?" Bob asked.

"I want to glorify God. I want to see people come to Jesus Christ—"

"Right! Those are results, not the focus. Can you see the difference? Who is your target audience? Who are the people you want to reach?"

"Why, everybody."

"Think about that some too. Also, what are you trying to say to them through your music?"

"That God loves them, that God forgives—"

"Still not focused," he said patiently. Because I liked and respected him, I listened to what he said. "Everybody won't like your music. No artist has universal appeal. You need to think it through, Roger, and decide who you want to reach—your primary target. Others will listen. Others will respond, but you need to focus on a particular group or type of people."

In retrospect, that sounds so obvious. But it wasn't obvious to me. Ask me the question today and I can tell you our demographics suggest that our audiences are largely in the sixteen-to-forty age range. Today we are a group that does churches, colleges, and denominational conventions.

Through questioning, nudging, and suggesting, Bob MacKenzie challenged me to consider who I was, who I wanted TRUTH to be, and especially what message I wanted to convey through TRUTH. This took me further than I ever would have gone on my own. I had good reason to respect Bob's experience and opinions. His interest and concern caused me to ask, *Do I want just to make music? Or do I want to have a vital ministry?* In my heart I wanted to have a ministry.

And as he so often did, Bob left the final decisions to me. I would be deciding what our focus was, who our particular audience would be. Just as I had already learned from Bob to pick out that "man on the third row," I learned from him now to focus our performances, not to take absolutely every opportunity that came along. I was still learning, however, to weigh my decisions carefully—to listen to people like Bob, but also to listen carefully to my own heart as well.

~

Recording and performing were not my only concerns in the glory years. I was feeling a growing sense of mission, a sense that God wanted to use TRUTH in other countries.

My first real opportunity for missions outside the United States came in 1976. While TRUTH was playing in the San Diego area, we had a free Sunday and drove across the border into Tiajuana, Mexico, to visit a small Pentecostal church. Three of our members— Steve Green, Art Ortiz, and Art's sister Jolene— spoke Spanish.

Between the dirt roads and holes as big as the front end of the bus, I didn't think we'd make it to the church. But we finally managed to maneuver our way around the hurdles. We set up at the church and did several numbers in English although the Spanish speakers in our group did most of the leading.

At the end of the service, we started to pack everything away. Just then the pastor came forward and spoke to the congregation in Spanish. Immediately they stretched out their hands toward us; all of them prayed aloud for us. Noisy it may have been, but I was moved by a powerful sense that these people were speaking to God from their hearts.

Then, to my surprise, the pastor insisted on taking an offering. As soon as the people had given, he nodded for Art Ortiz to interpret for him. "This is a love gift for you." He handed me the money.

"Oh, no," I said, touched at their generosity and aware of how little they had and the poverty in which they lived. "We didn't come for that. We can't take their money."

"You must take the money," Art whispered. "This is a gift of love. These people will be very hurt if you don't take their love gift."

Inwardly I wanted to cry at the sacrifice I knew that some of them must be making. Instead I smiled as broadly as I could, and I thanked them and the pastor (with Art interpreting for me).

At the end of the service, we packed everything in the bus, and the congregation milled around. I'll never forget those Mexican Christians, standing around the church, holding up their hands, again praying for us as we left. *Thank you, God,* I prayed silently as we drove away. *Thank you for their kindness to us.* They ministered to us far more than we could possibly have blessed them. These poor Christians gave us much more than money. We tend to give out of our affluence, but they showed sacrificial giving.

For a long time I thought of that worship service, and it warmed my heart as I realized that we could minister to them through music even when they didn't understand English. God had planted the seed of the vision, and it would grow.

~

Ups and downs. Joys and heartaches. And through it all the mission of TRUTH. Every day brought a new crisis, a new challenge. I knew so little when I went out on the road; I learned something new every day. Some wonderful songs came from those glorious years. People were listening, learning who TRUTH was.

I was doing the best I could. And I'll always be thankful God chose to use me!

Chapter 5

A Moment of Change

It seemed as if *nothing* was going right in 1976.

"I'm just not sure what to do," I said to my brother Billy. "I need to be in Wichita by tonight, but I don't know if I ought to leave." Billy understood and so did Dad.

Mother was dying.

It was early fall. TRUTH, along with other groups and individuals like Doug Oldham and Bob MacKenzie, were scheduled to shoot a movie in Wichita, Kansas. Billy Zeoli of Gospel Films was making a biographical salute to John W. Peterson, who penned many wonderful hymns.

For five years I'd flown home many times, convinced it was the last time I'd see Mother alive. TRUTH was scheduled for filming the next day. All the kids were there, but I was in Mobile.

I spent most of the day in the hospital at my mother's bedside, flooded with childhood memories. She was a strong and beautiful woman. Whenever she came to my elementary school, my friends wouldn't believe she was my mother: "She can't be your mother—she's too beautiful."

As I thought of my beautiful mother, I felt bad that I was away so much. And I had real turmoil at the same time. On the one hand, I felt I was never with Mom enough. At the same time, I felt guilty for being away so much from TRUTH, especially right then. Some things were going on that demanded my attention. I felt pulled to go and pressed to stay.

After struggling over the matter most of the day and seeing no change in Mom, I decided to catch the last flight to Wichita. After saying good-bye to everyone, I left the hospital room, started walking down the hallway, and then slowly descended the stairs. Yet with each step I felt increasingly troubled.

"This just isn't right," I said aloud. "I can't leave."

Turning around, I walked back down the hall to Mom's room. Then I saw Dad and Billy. Dad's eyes met mine and instantly I knew: my mother was gone. *She's gone. She's gone.* For a few minutes nothing else got through to me. My sister, Debby, ran to a stairway to be alone—her heart broken.

Later I did call ahead, and TRUTH filmed the segment without me. I was where I needed to be. For more than five years I had watched my mother fade away with cancer. Linda had pitched in to help as much as she could while I was away, and more than once I thought of the relief we would share when her pain was finally over. Yet when Mother actually died, it hurt terribly.

My tears flowed, and the family gathered to share the sorrow and to comfort one another. In her weakened condition, Mother had cared enough to write a letter, which we read after she died. I thought of the death of Jacob in the Old Testament. On his deathbed, he called in each of his sons and spoke to them individually. Mother had done the same for all of us, by writing to us.

The pain of losing her seemed intensified by the fact that I was already unhappy with myself and having difficulty with TRUTH. One particular member of TRUTH was causing confusion and disruption. He grumbled and never seemed satisfied. He talked to others, and they soon grumbled about things that ordinarily wouldn't have bothered them: One complaining spirit becomes contagious.

When I rejoined TRUTH after Mom's funeral, my first administrative decision was to call the young man aside and ask him to leave, a tough decision to make. On top of the difficulties with the group, I was going through a professional crisis. My grief over Mom was intensified, and my conflict over TRUTH's direction was brought to a head when I remembered that Mom had always worried that we'd get a little bit too loud and a little too rocky.

I had always had Mom's comment in the back of my mind as I planned our program, but a year or so earlier a subtle change had crept in. A "new sound" was appearing in Christian music, and I have never been one to fall behind.

The change in TRUTH's performances became apparent as a result of a conversation in Nashville.

"Roger, let's try something different," said one of my friends there. "Maybe the Abba sound. You could really make it, Roger. I know you could."

"You think so?" I asked. "I have heard of the Swedish group, but I've never thought of trying to sound like them."

"I don't mean to imitate them," my friend said. "Use their sound as a guide. Observe them. Listen to their style. You could do worse. A lot worse." My friends in Nashville were talking to me about what they called the Abba sound because the group was making big money and drawing record-breaking crowds in a tour of the world. A number of secular groups had already copied the Abba sound. "You'd reach a lot more people," he said. I never questioned their sincerity, and they certainly were not trying to hurt my career.

"Maybe that's what I ought to do," I said.

These men knew their business and hadn't misled me for the years we had been recording for the Benson label. I was willing to try anything if it made us a better group. Their ideas had always worked before—especially when they helped us in selecting songs. I had introduced a Gaither song called "The Church Triumphant" throughout the South, and people responded overwhelmingly to the way we brought life to that number.

During those years I was still insecure. I was in contact with leaders in Christian music and didn't know where my own opinions fit into the picture. I was still trying to find out who we were. Instead of deciding who we were and what we sounded like, I kept trying to make TRUTH into whatever I thought the important people around me wanted us to be. It would take me a long, long time to realize that when we try to be who we aren't, we end up confused and sometimes brokenhearted.

We were moving along; more doors were opening. Yet I felt as if I were going through some kind of identity crisis. Maybe I was really struggling over not wanting to be just another cover group. Yet by any criterion, TRUTH was successful. We were making good music and training a lot of extremely talented young people. I loved what we were doing.

In those days we called our style "contemporary Christian music"—the popular sounds of the 1970s. In the church it had started as a soft pop or soft rock; in the ensuing years the sound got a little harder and little more rocky. While the turmoil raged inside me, the top people at the Benson Company kept challenging me to change our image. One of them said, "Roger, you're on the cutting edge of Christian music in the church. You need to take the next step." They had helped me to make contacts and had done so much for us. I felt I owed them something. After all, they had guided me so skillfully; it seemed only natural that they would know what we should do next.

For what happened afterward, I don't blame the people at Benson. I'm a responsible adult and I should have been praying and asking God for guidance. Not that I didn't ask God—I did—I just wasn't listening to the answers.

In late 1976, we decided to be on the cutting edge

of church music. I honestly believed we were because the powerful voices at Benson had said so. They stroked my ego by saying things like, "Roger, you're doing great work. People are listening to you. You've got the ability to move the church forward musically." I assumed they knew the music-buying public better than I did. It didn't occur to me that they might be wrong. A revitalized TRUTH was enjoying the flush of success with high attendance and new doors opening to us all the time. These were good days, so I assumed I had been so well accepted that I could move a little further musically. *Why stay with the same forty standards?* I asked myself. Let the people hear the new music. We've built up our following; now we're ready to take them forward. My reasoning sounded fine to my own ears. Yet it was a mistake—a mistake that would take years to rectify.

I've always done a potpourri of music. In our concerts we begin with fun and praise numbers—like having the audience clap or sing along with us—and then present a few contemporary numbers, something upbeat. I've always tried to be sensitive to the fact that adults as well as kids attended. That affects the style of music. Teens seem to like it loud, hard, and experimental. We were playing to a diverse audience, often more older adults than youth. By late 1975 and especially during 1976 I had grown overly confident. "I'm going to take these people a little further in music," I told our kids. "People can learn and they can change." While that may be true, nobody appointed me as their agent of change. But I didn't think about that. I just jumped in and decided to help people move on whether they liked it or not.

This change in our music happened gradually. Had anyone followed us around the country for several months, they might not have noticed much deviation from our beginning sound. But those who didn't hear us for at least a year could tell the difference.

During our concerts, I've tried to make our music say, "Here's who we are." In my ignorance, I tried to say something more. Without actually using these words, I was communicating this message: "We've been out in the real world, and we know what's going on. We travel among a wide range of church people, and we know what you need whether you recognize that or not. We're going to do this music for you because it's what you need."

At the same time, Linda was softly saying things like, "Roger, do you think you ought to use that song? Is the music covering up the words?" But I wasn't listening to her either. I even wished she could be just a little more supportive instead of questioning all the time. A few friends said, "You're moving into rock and roll, aren't you?" Or "You sound like the music of the world, Roger, instead of the people of God." They didn't know what was happening in our country, so I wasn't listening to them either.

I *was* listening to several members of TRUTH who wanted to rock. Soon the beat and power of the instruments overpowered the words of the songs. That's one thing Linda mentioned several times— never in a pushy way but expressive of how she felt. "You might be defeating the purpose of why you're out there if the music distorts the message and people can't hear the words." But I still wasn't listening. I discussed issues like style, lyrics, the movement, the type of songs—just to show her how open I was. Actually I wanted to educate her and to bring her around to my way of thinking.

Perhaps deep down inside I did hear Linda and the friendly critics, but I thought I knew what I was doing. TRUTH had become successful, and my commitment and hard work had been at the heart of that success. People liked us. Bookings were coming in. My attitude to Linda and to others was really saying, "I understand what you're talking about, but you have to trust me. I'm making the right decision about taking the church the next step." I had become a crusader and was out to reform and to teach the church about new music.

I'd always tried to be open, believing that if something is working elsewhere, it ought to work for me. Our producers called TRUTH a "cover tune" group, which meant that some other group was already using the same songs, but we also would record them. For example, Bill Gaither was writing and recording his own music, but we were recording it as well, using our distinctive sound. Both of us were selling records, but we were doing more concerts. I got so self-confident I believed that we could do Gaither music better than Gaither himself. However, he sold more records and had larger crowds. For consolation, I reminded myself that the author of the tune will naturally attract more people than some group using the music.

While trying to develop the kind of program we felt would work, I constantly listened to other groups and observed the results. If I felt that something was working for them, it could, with slight modification, work for me. I didn't mind saying, "Hey, let's put this tune in our program." And we did.

~

But we still had a lesson to learn—to stop copying others and to develop our own style. Since TRUTH wasn't the Benson Recording Company's leading artist, we didn't often get the best songs. Throughout those years, I not only took TRUTH on tour, but I was also out there selling records and tapes. Benson actually makes more money through TRUTH than through some of the major names because of my efforts to promote our recordings and the number of annual concerts we do. More people come to our concerts than ever walk into a record store. So the people at Benson liked me because I worked a lot. Had we been a weekend group, they would have dropped us quickly. Instead of averaging two concerts a week the way some of the big names do, we did—and still do—nine or ten each week.

When I finally woke up and saw how much I had veered in the wrong direction musically as I adapted TRUTH's sound, I wanted to blame someone else. It seemed easy just to call our audiences closedminded.

Armed with a new album we completed in Hollywood, using a new and different sound, we tried to take the church further musically than the church was ready or willing to go. We came close to being a rock-and-roll group. For this I paid a price. And it has haunted me for years.

We had introduced those great Gaither songs like "Because He Lives," and "The Church Triumphant." The young people in the audience identified with us and responded, but I confused many of the other people by the songs, style, and sounds of a TRUTH they didn't recognize. For instance, one song on our new album *A Funny Thing Happened on the Way to Hell (I Got Saved, Saved, Saved)*. Quite a switch from songs like "Because He Lives."

By 1978 we had our smallest group ever—thirteen people—and even they were confused. Despite their uncertainties, those young people stood on the platform, singing and playing with all their hearts—that's what was winning for TRUTH. I didn't really appreciate them enough. I was in terrible turmoil because I didn't know whom to trust or what to do.

Audiences let me know in dozens of ways that they didn't like what we had done. The phone didn't ring as often. Our return engagements, on which we depended, went down. A few talked behind my back, but a number of them spoke their feelings to my face.

God had given me the responsibility for a full-time group, and I had foolishly assumed that making it successful rested on being like all the other groups out there. "It's got to be slick," I had said several times.

And it *was* slick. Well thought out. The problem is, it wasn't me. Consequently, we received a tremendous amount of criticism. At first I defended myself (even if I didn't say it out loud). But then I reminded myself that even *I* wasn't at home or at peace with who TRUTH had become.

In those days, I figured out all kinds of ways to justify myself.

The picture wasn't totally bleak. In 1977 our calendar was full, including a seventeen-day tour of Europe and eight days in Jamaica. During this time we were busy, but I was feeling in my heart we were not communicating with our audience. Our original intention to communicate the gospel through our music was being overridden by the new sound.

"TRUTH is too rock and roll for our church." That statement probably best summarizes the attitude of many toward TRUTH from mid-1975 through early 1978. Those were our most difficult days. Yet, even then, I wasn't ready to admit how bad it was. We started going downhill, and I didn't know what to do to change our direction. Our singers and instrumentalists got discouraged, and several left us. I still didn't catch on. At one point we dropped down to three horns and three singers: our keyboard player (Eddie Anders) had to double up as a singer. I was still pushing this new sound for TRUTH. The fact is, we were dying spiritually and financially. Among the remaining group members, we didn't have the rapport that had been such a significant part of TRUTH. I couldn't figure out what to do.

Beyond admitting, "We're at a crisis point," I remained as bewildered as everyone else. Linda was hurting for me; she was also praying for me. Maybe she still tried to help, but I couldn't have heard anything. Christmas of 1978 was coming up soon, and I kept thinking, *We'll have a couple of weeks' rest. Things will feel better after a rest.* In the meantime, we stayed with our scheduled concerts. In a kind of inner desperation, I finally started looking inward and talking to God. I knew that God had called me down a road to do a specific task, but on the journey I had detoured and gotten lost. I was miserable.

Obviously I had failed—although no one ever specifically said that.

Nothing was working right, and gradually I accepted the blame and started questioning myself. *Am I good enough to lead this group? To lead any group? Am I doing the right thing? Have I dishonored God by what I've been doing?* No answers came. I was hurting, everything was crumbling around me, and I couldn't get a handle on anything.

Then I remembered something said to me by an intelligent young man who had joined TRUTH. I explained my role to him: "You won't call me by my first name. I won't be your buddy, but I'd like to be the best friend you have if there is anything you ever need." I explained why I felt it was important to remain apart and that somebody had to say yes or no and make decisions. My concluding statement was, "I want you to know that I'm the director and the leader of this group."

He listened to everything I said. When I finished, he looked up and said, "Let me say one thing to you. I don't have any problem with your being the leader of this group, but I want you to know this one thing. If you're the leader, be sure you lead me or I'll get nervous."

As I looked back over the past months, I realized I had led TRUTH to this difficult era of ministry. I didn't like where I'd led them.

In 1971 TRUTH had started by singing in the little churches. My plan was to go from the small congregations to the biggies and the college auditoriums and the civic centers and, finally, on to the stadiums. *Shouldn't we be out there in the big places, drawing immense crowds? I wondered. What's happened to the line of progressions? Then I realized, Hey, I'm a church man. In the churches is where I belong until God shows me differently.*

Right at that time one of our singers, Kim Noblitt, walked up to me and began a conversation that would help change everything. "Mr. B.," he said, "I'm troubled about something, and I want to talk it over with you."

"Sure, Kim," I said, priding myself on always being open with people and being able to listen to them. Deep concern showed on his face, and I wondered if he was having personal problems, maybe a sad love affair or money troubles. "It's like this. When I came here I thought I was going to be part of TRUTH." He paused and took a deep breath. "This group I'm with right now isn't the TRUTH I heard at Estes Park, [Colorado], at the big conference. Why did you have to change TRUTH? I loved TRUTH the way it was."

His words stunned me; I tried to recover by saying, "Uh, well, Kim, we've been trying to find our own voice."

"TRUTH already had a voice. A great voice. That's why I wanted to work with you, Mr. B. But this!" He shook his head. "I want to tell you something: This isn't TRUTH."

I didn't say much after that because he spoke the

very words I needed to hear. Finally I forced myself to smile, and I thanked him. "You know what, Kim? We're going to have TRUTH again. And soon!"

I began to listen to my own heart and returned to the right path by deciding to be the person God had called me to be. That meant that I would lead TRUTH in my own leadership style.

Others had said words very like Kim's—at least they tried to. Several times Linda had gently tried to tell me I was wrong, but I never really listened. Other voices had spoken, but I convinced myself that they didn't know the situation as well as I did. By the end of 1978, however, I was so frustrated that I was finally ready for an answer from anybody. When Kim said, "This isn't TRUTH," the words stung. He was right. We weren't TRUTH, and we weren't any of the groups we imitated or followed. Only one answer loomed before me: We had to go back to who we were.

Kim talked to me on December 3, 1978. After our conversation, I abruptly ended our tour. *I'm going to find TRUTH again*, I said to myself—*the original TRUTH*.

God spoke to me through Kim, and as I followed up and made changes, I sensed I was going in the right direction again. God was telling me to be Roger Breland.

And, perhaps for the first time in my life, it felt okay just to be me. I wasn't Abba; I wasn't a groovy rocker—and I didn't have to be anybody else. It was all right to be me. It was okay for me to be a church guy who led a group of young singers in the church.

Kim had confronted me at exactly the right time

because I had set up TRUTH so that we had two long breaks twice in the year—in late June and mid-December.

I told the group, "We're not going to do any more concerts. We're returning to Mobile, and we're going to stay there until TRUTH sounds the way it used to." Rather than trying to change the kids we had with us, I decided to start over. Kim, who had been with us only a few months, stayed on along with two others, but I released the rest of them. (Actually Kim stayed with TRUTH for eight years. He remained a source of immense blessing to TRUTH and to me personally.)

From my file of names, I contacted prospects. Most of them, excited to be contacted, auditioned for me. I talked with John Coates, a top arranger. "John, I need you. I want you to help us arrange music so that TRUTH sounds right—the way it used to." John came to Mobile, became our staff arranger, and worked hard during that transition. Soon I had the music we needed.

On December 26, 1978, I began rehearsals with a new group. We were moving back to the old sound and the old look of *TRUTH*. And it felt good to know I was moving in that direction again. During the two and a half weeks we had off for Christmas, we rehearsed so that TRUTH could be back on the road the first of January. With our new crew we let everyone hear the old TRUTH sound.

For the next few years we concentrated on rebuilding and recovering. We had to build confidence and restore trust. In some ways, it was like starting over. But we were moving in the right direction. That's what counted.

The first concert we did was at the annual Inter-Varsity missions conference for Christian college students in Urbana, Illinois—a wonderful opportunity to sing to thousands of young adults. We were terrible—at least it seemed that way to me. The group wasn't yet ready. A lot of people thought we were great, but I knew what we could be—I knew what we would be—again.

Not good yet, I admitted, *but we're on our way*. The fire was lit again. My excitement grew and the ideas flowed through my mind. We'd become the TRUTH of old—only better. Sure, I'd made mistakes—plenty of them—but now I was ready to make the right decisions.

Chapter 6

A Moment of Recovery

We went on the road with the revitalized TRUTH. Most people opened their arms and welcomed us as we moved back to the way we had been. Over the years, we've more than redeemed ourselves.

The climb back wasn't always easy. Even today, we still have a few painful memories. One especially painful rejection took place when the Southern Baptist's annual convention went to New Orleans in 1980. The leaders had invited TRUTH to sing at a meeting for pastors. Realizing the importance of this convention, we arranged a package of new songs. We even bought new clothes for everyone.

Our audience would be thousands of pastors. We were offering the kind of music I knew they'd like and were ready to provide one of the best packages I'd ever put together. An hour before the midday meeting, our bus pulled up in front of the hotel, which was the concert site, and started to unload.

Just about that time, a well-known evangelist saw us, said something to the kids unloading, and demanded to know where I was. "Inside," one of them said and went on with his work. The evangelist got on the bus and demanded, "Where's the leader of this outfit?"

"I'm Roger Breland," I said. Although we'd never met before, I did know who he was.

"We're not going to have that kind of music here! I want to tell you that much right now!"

"Well, sir," I said, "we've been invited to sing—"

"I'm the leader of this pastor's meeting. I'll tell you something right now. You will not sing because I won't let you. We don't like your rock music—I suppose you call it music—"

"If you'd let me explain—"

"I don't need an explanation. I just want you out of here!"

"Look, we're not here to cause any confusion. We were invited and—"

"Then I'm uninviting you! I refuse to have you appear on our program!"

Ordinarily I would have tried again to talk to him, to find out what was really troubling him. But the answer in his voice and the shrillness of his tones told me it would only infuriate him more. He did admit that he had never heard TRUTH sing. "In that case, sir," I said, keeping my temper in check with a maximum of willpower, "we'll just get on the bus and leave."

"I think that's the best solution," he said, and he stormed off the bus. When someone asked why we didn't sing at the pastor's meeting, he announced that he had asked me to leave because I didn't have "a good spirit." Several hours later a friend called us to say he could get us back on the program. It was too late to work the details out.

That might have been the end of this story, but the ending actually came several years later when that same evangelist and I met again. He mentioned the incident: "Roger, I'm sorry for what happened. I apologize." As he spoke, I remembered the verse Dr. Ritchie had given me a decade earlier—1 Thessalonians 2:4: "But as we have been approved of God to be entrusted with the gospel, even so we speak, not as pleasing men, but God who tests our hearts." Of course I accepted his apology. I also realized he had no idea how deeply he had hurt us, especially at a time when we were struggling just to survive.

Those conventions were important because the pastors came from all over America. Had they been able to hear us and if they had liked us, they could have opened many doors for us. Since his apology, I've also received a warm letter from him, thanking TRUTH for its ministry.

Some people who heard us in 1976 still won't believe anything good about us. I recall one pastor in Houston, Texas, who phoned me. "You're doing all of this rock and roll, satanic music. I don't like it, and I want you to know I don't like it. And I want you to know that I'll never allow you to come to our church!" For ten minutes he gave it to me.

"You're exactly right, and I'm sorry," I said but he cut me off. Four times during the conversation I tried to apologize, but he wouldn't listen. I didn't try to defend myself or TRUTH, and I finally even stopped trying to apologize because he was absolutely unreasonable. He didn't want to hear anything from me; he just wanted to go on a tirade. A few days later I received a letter from him—what I called a genuine hate letter, the worst I've ever received. He repeated basically what he had said before and added, "I intend to write to all of the Baptist leadership in the state of Texas and urge them to boycott you. I hope and I pray that you'll never get a chance to play anywhere again in this state." (So far as I know he never wrote them. Or if he did, enough of the leaders must have known what a mean-spirited man he was and didn't pay much attention.)

After getting the letter, I phoned, but he wouldn't speak to me. I called back the next day, and he still wouldn't talk to me. I managed to talk with the youth pastor and asked him to give the senior minister my apology. I never heard from the pastor again. An interesting after-the-fact piece of information is that within months, this church experienced serious problems. It had been a big congregation, but he was a man filled with hatred, and churches don't grow without love and fellowship. Their attendance fell drastically, and it still took the church a long time to start growing again after he resigned. As I thought of that pastor, I recall saying to Linda, "In the very places where we speak of forgiveness, understanding, and loving, sometimes we never have the chance to receive them."

Another sad rejection involves an evangelist who spoke at a luncheon in my home church. Obviously he didn't know we had any connections with that congregation. Linda was present and heard him ranting against other groups and people. "There's a group right here in your own town called TRUTH. God's not going to use it." He said several negative things about us, as well as about other Christian ministries.

Later, my pastor spoke up. "I don't know what you've heard about Roger Breland and TRUTH. But we know TRUTH here, and we love him, and we know those things aren't true." The evangelist admitted he didn't know us personally, but had heard of us years before. He had gotten his information from someone he highly respected. This evangelist later came to a concert and thanked us for our ministry.

I could cite other examples, but I don't want to give the impression that everyone was against us—although in my dark moments, it seemed that way.

All through 1979 and 1980 I was waiting—often wondering if TRUTH would survive. I didn't just wait, though. I worked hard. While I tried to rebuild TRUTH, finances reached the disaster level.

Our brief attempt at changing our style was not the only reason for the financial difficulties. Obviously we *had* confused the churches, and they still needed reassurance that the old TRUTH was back. But other factors were at work. About that time America went into a recession. Oil prices soared, and inflation raced up into double digits. Our expenses were at an all-time high while our income was at a low point.

On the other side of our recovery experience, though, I found great comfort when I returned home and shared special times with Linda and the boys. The boys were never the "gimme this, gimme that" type. And Linda and I were always honest with them as TRUTH went through the struggles of the late seventies. Since I've always wanted to do a little extra for them to make up for being gone so much of the time, their ability to keep pressure off me felt like a wonderful gift of grace.

It always gave me great joy to do special things with them—a trip to New York City, for example. When we really couldn't do special things that cost money, we got just as much pleasure out of the tradition of the red plate.

Linda and I learned early that dinner together is a special family time. She made dinner special for the boys even while I was away. And when I was home, I was eager to help make dinner a memorable occasion. The red plate shows up at dinner time—always at the place of a person whose presence at the table is a cause for celebration that day. Often, when I came home from a road trip, weary and sometimes discouraged, I found the red plate at my place and felt the welcoming, joyous love of my wife and sons.

Whenever I could, I found reasons to put the red plate at someone else's place—good grades, a graduation, an award, mastering a new skill. I was and am proud of my family. Not everyone can claim that his family rejoiced with him during the hard times as well as the glory days.

The traditions of our family life always brought us pleasure in difficult times. We have come to realize that God has used our being apart so much to bring all of us closer together.

Sometimes as I wrote "I love you" in shaving cream on Linda's mirror or sent her flowers, I felt that, whatever problems faced me outside our home,

Linda, age 5, and her brother, Buddy, age 3.

A moment of youth: Linda Guernsey at age 2.

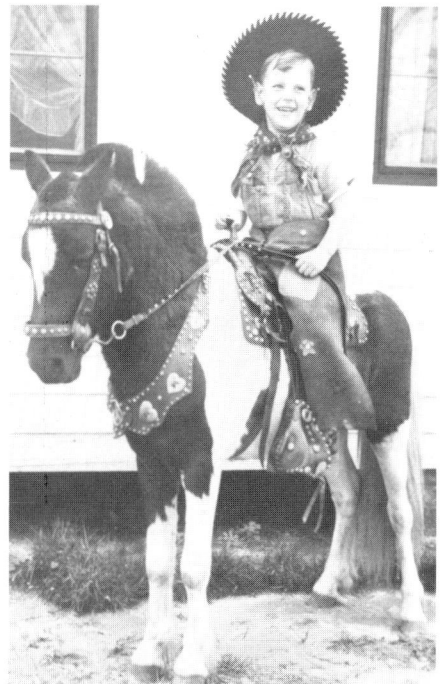

Above: Roger in front of Mount Calvary Baptist Church at age 10.

Left: Roger plays a young cowboy at age 3, in Biloxi, Mississippi.

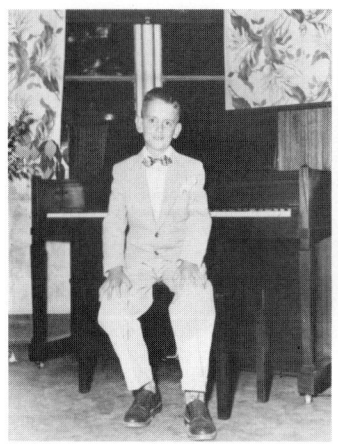

His first suit and his first piano recital: Roger in third grade.

By his junior year in high school, music was a major part of his life. Here Roger plays trumpet in a stage band.

A senior at Vigor High School, Roger was a drum major.

Roger and Linda were college sweethearts at Troy State. They never dated anyone else after their first date their freshman year.

Roger and Linda married September 12, 1964. Because he was not yet 21, Roger had to have his father's permission for the marriage license.

Linda Guernsey 1964: her engagement picture.

Roger organized both Varsity (left photo) and Spring Hill Singers (above) in his first years at Spring Hill Baptist Church in Mobile, Alabama. The formation of these groups helped Roger understand how to combine a big band with a choir, all to proclaim the message of Jesus Christ. And this led to the birth of TRUTH.

Roger and the boys, (from left) John, Jason, Jeremy.

(From left) Jason, John, and Jeremy, Christmas 1973. It was difficult to leave the boys to go on the road. Roger never stopped missing them.

TRUTH, 1972

TRUTH, 1976

Roger receives the Gold Sales Award from The Benson Company. (Left to right)
Jerry Parks, general manager and CEO of Benson, Roger Breland, and
Dan Cleary, A & R director.

Above: Jason "on the mike" on the
TRUTH bus, 1974.

At right: Jason "on the mike" with
TRUTH, the 1989 cruise.

TRUTH in Jamica, 1977. Although the group was busy during this time, they enjoyed the rapport as they communicated with their audience.

TRUTH, 1979.

John was married to a beautiful young woman, Tracy Key, December 30, 1989.

One of the group's most exciting ventures overseas: TRUTH in the Philippines, January, 1989. This trip revitalized the group's desire to take the message of Christ to other countries. Top and bottom photos: At the school concert the first morning, 3400 attended; 1700 made decisions for Christ.

Although the group's style has changed through the years, the message remains the same: Trust and Receive Unchangeable True Happiness in Jesus.

TRUTH, 1989

TRUTH, 1992

TRUTH, 1996

Breland family photo, 1992. Front row (left to right) Roger, Linda, Jason. Top row (left to right) Jeremy, John, Tracy and Elizabeth.

Jeremy was married to lovely Jennifer Blomstrom, June 18, 1994.

In a story-book wedding Amy Leigh Thames became Mrs. Jason Ross Breland on January 7, 1995.

TRUTH in concert at a Russian military base in Moscow. Pastor Tom Mullins spoke and over half of the soldiers made decisions for Christ. Each one received a Bible.

Russian soldiers presented TRUTH flowers following the concert.

An open air concert in Timasoara, Romania. Hundreds of students died in this plaza during the Revolution.

TRUTH gave a concert at the train station in Budapest, Hungary. Several hundred prayed to receive Jesus.

(Fron left to right) Bill Breland, Pastor Peter Vidu, Emanuel Baptist Church, Oradea, Romania, and Roger.

Integrity presented an award for TRUTH'S four "Top Ten Songs" 1994-1995. (From left to right) Don Moen, Wendell Gafford, Glen Wagner, Roger Breland, Jason Breland and Chris Thomason.

Roger speaks to staff at the Orphanage in Borisov, Belarus, August 1995.

Jason and Amy Breland with TRUTH at Minsk Prison, Minsk, Belarus August 1995.

Sparkling white 45-foot TRUTH bus, 1996.

Grand-pa's Brag Book

Grand-daughters
Elizabeth Rose
and
Caroline Olivia,
1995.

Grandpa and Nana with
Elizabeth and Caroline,
Christmas night, 1995.

*Happy "1st" Birthday,
Caroline Olivia, May 1996.*

*Pretty Elizabeth Rose,
May 1996.*

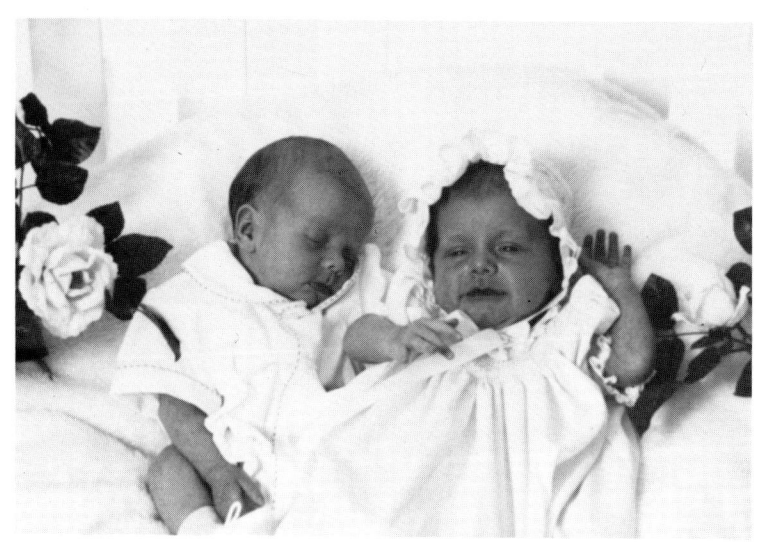

John Roger III and Anna Victoria, May 1996

(From left to right) Caroline, John, Anna, and Elizabeth

inside our home I would find romance and security and steadfast commitment and support.

~

I found more encouragement as God's work in the lives of TRUTH members began to reveal itself.

Just before the end of 1980, Michael Wells came back into my life. Mike, who went with the first tour of TRUTH in 1971, had sung in my youth choir at Spring Hill Baptist Church in the tenth grade. He was with me in choir for three years in high school and two years on the road with TRUTH. Maybe because he grew up in a single-parent home, I was the closest to a dad he ever knew.

After two years with TRUTH, Michael wanted to spread his wings a little, and get away from me— which is natural. But at the time, I was a little possessive and wanted him to hang around. I felt disappointed and let down when he left.

Michael married and went off to New York to study at the Mannes School of Music. Later he messed up his life and plunged into alcohol. One day, his wife announced she was leaving with their son. His life was in total disarray. For at least seven years I never saw or heard of Michael, but I never forgot him.

Occasionally I asked people who had known him, "Ever hear anything of Mike Wells?" Then someone told me that he had moved to New Orleans, and I heard stories about what had happened. I grieved for Mike because I still cared for him.

In early 1981 when I looked him up, Mike was

managing a music store in New Orleans. Since TRUTH was doing a concert in the area, I pleaded with him to come and hear us. Michael came, but he sat on the back row. He observed from a fairly critical perspective, I suppose, because he knew so much about TRUTH and everything that went into a concert. After all, he was not only musically talented, but he had been with us at the inception of TRUTH in 1971.

After the concert, he and I went out to eat. TRUTH was preparing for a ten-year reunion, and all former members were invited to come back and have a special time together. I begged Michael to come too.

"I don't know," he kept saying over and over. I couldn't leave Michael that night and felt strongly that I needed to stay with him. New Orleans is close enough to Mobile that I had planned to drive on home afterward; instead I asked if I could spend the night at his place. Mike agreed.

We kept talking until about two-thirty in the morning, when Michael began to weep. God had gotten through to him. We prayed together and he cried some more. He also agreed to attend the reunion. He had been afraid that if he came, those from TRUTH who knew how he had messed up his life might make fun of him. I promised him that they wouldn't. (And, of course, they didn't.) When Michael turned up on the first day of the three-day event, I challenged him, "You need to get right with God again and obey whatever he wants you to do."

He didn't say much, mostly things like, "I'm trying, Roger. I'm trying to get it sorted out."

On the second day of the reunion, Michael tapped

me on the shoulder and called me aside. "I don't know what I'm going to do," he said.

"About what?" I asked, realizing what he was talking about from the pained expression on his face.

"I don't know what God wants me to do, Roger. But I do want you to know that He's got my attention. I have a thirty-thousand-dollar-a-year job in New Orleans. I'm going back next week and resign. Then I'm coming to Mobile. I don't know what I'm going to do here, but I know this is where I have to start."

"You can start out with TRUTH until you know more clearly."

"You mean that?" he asked in amazement. "You mean you'd have me back again?"

"Absolutely."

Michael resigned his job and joined TRUTH for the second time. He stayed for two years. Mike is a talented man: he's an arranger, writer, keyboard player, and brass instrumentalist. For two years in 1982–1983, he was the leader of my group. While TRUTH was on the road, he met and later married a fine Christian girl. They moved to Nashville where he got a job as an arranger. He was later employed by Thomas Road Baptist Church in Lynchburg, Virginia.

~

At the close of those difficult, rocky, rebuilding years, the 1980 TRUTH workshop in Mobile was a spiritual high with three hundred people attending. Using the facilities of the University of South Alabama in Mobile, TRUTH sponsored a three-day workshop for people who wanted to be involved in ministries like TRUTH. We brought in groups and personalities from all over the country: musicians, such as Ronn Huff, John Coates, Steven V. Taylor, Larnelle Harris—and speakers, such as Ron Dunn and our pastor, Dr. Fred Wolfe.

While I used this workshop to search for new talent, the overall purpose was to assist people who were interested in ministering with groups like TRUTH. We selected five directors, assigned each a group, and added a rhythm section; then they rehearsed during the day. At the end of the week they performed for the rest of us.

Each day from eight in the morning until four in the afternoon, we held a variety of classes on everything in music education from arranging and vocals to brass and using sound equipment. At night we featured a major concert artist or group, including TRUTH, and ended each evening with a dynamic message from Ron Dunn, who was our spiritual emphasis speaker. We even made up and sold T-shirts that said "I Survived the TRUTH Workshop in 1980."

The last night we put all the groups together and did a finale. That was some singing, and I understood what people meant when they said they thought the roof would fly away. It was a wonderful experience, a great week musically and spiritually. TRUTH had turned around. Maybe everybody didn't know it, but I did. Not only were lives being changed among those who came to see us, but I was again seeing growth among TRUTH members. At our ten-year reunion memories swept over me as I thought of "graduates" of TRUTH who were reaching across the world to change lives. One of my greatest joys over the years has been to see how God has used and continues to use each one of these members from the first year as well as the hundreds that have followed in the footsteps.

Marty Feazell and Joe Estes are married and have two children. Joe is the minister of music in a large church in Fayetteville, Georgia. Marty still does special projects with TRUTH, such as chairing the organization of the TRUTH twentieth reunion. Donna Taylor is married and has a lovely family in North Alabama, and she has faced a real difficulty for one who loves music—becoming deaf. Jan Stevens still lives in Mobile and is a vocal instructor. Buddy Hornaday, our "Mr. Personality," now uses the name Byron Day in his work as a television personality. He lives in Mobile with his wife, Kim, and two children. Both Ed and Fred Sharrett have married and are still very much involved with the ministry in the Atlanta area.

Two of our first members went on to the mission field. Fern Strait, her husband, and their children are missionaries in Chile. Gary and Sharon Hannie and their children are missionaries in Mexico. Gary graduated from Samford and then Southern Seminary and was a minister of music before God did a deep work in his heart, placing him on the mission field.

Mike Wells is a minister of music and lives with his wife, Pam, and their children in Atlanta. Vince Harris is finishing his doctor of music degree in Hattiesburg, Mississippi, where he lives with his wife and family. Ricky Spears, his wife Becky, and their two children live in Memphis, Tennessee, where Ricky is a successful businessman. They are very actively involved in their church.

Kathy Taylor married Bert Youngblood, and they have four wonderful children. Bert is minister of music in Troy, Alabama. Kathy is still playing keyboard. Jerome Gilmer and his family live in Denver, Colorado, where he is a successful arranger and record producer. Mark Hardy and his wife are back in Paris, Texas, where Mark is associate pastor in a church. Steve Burks and his family have been successful in business in Birmingham, Alabama. And Gordon Twist lives in New York City and has even made it to Broadway. He still writes and arranges for TRUTH and helps us to produce albums.

As I looked at other instrumentalists of TRUTH I thought of John Morrell from a Roman Catholic background who surrendered his life to Jesus Christ while we were on the road. Since his days with TRUTH, John has been to Africa with the Wycliffe Bible Translators. Today he works on their psychological staff. During those three special days of reunion, I thought of so many former members of TRUTH, whom we still consider part of our family. As I looked at them, I couldn't help but remember when I first met them and where they had gone since. Neal Joseph, a wonderful young man who traveled with us in 1976, is vice president of a major recording label.

TRUTH also has its share of the unsung heroes—those who were never on stage—don't make the news or become well known, but are just as committed to God as any of the others. I think particularly of Larry Wright, our one-time bus driver. Larry supports himself driving buses for Greyhound, saves his money, and then takes a leave of absence to work in missions. He and his wife, Jo, have worked on the *Mercy Ship* in Central America and done missionary service in Guatemala. Along with their two children, they have lived in one room in Central America for months at a time—because of their burden for the people.

I had been saddened in those couple of years when TRUTH moved from its beginnings because I wasn't seeing the members move forward. But I also admitted that they didn't have much of an example to follow either. When we went back on the road, we concentrated on getting bookings in churches. We did colleges and conventions as well when the opportunities came, but even there we gave them the old (but improved) look and sound. Concerts were fun again. And a bigger boost was yet to come.

~

"I've got a song for TRUTH to record. You'll love it!" Steve said. "It's one of those songs that's been floating around, and nobody else has done it. This song is just the kind that fits TRUTH."

"Roger, I know you're going to love this one," Steve said. He sang a few bars. Then I got excited. First, I trusted Steve's sense of what fits TRUTH. Second, I trusted his musical sense. And third, we were looking for songs others hadn't already recorded.

The song had been floating around Nashville for a year. Some young man who worked in a Kansas City convenience store wrote it. The top artists passed it by, and then Steve found it. It was called "Jesus Never Fails," and it would become our biggest seller for the next decade. Steve soon put together enough of the right kind of songs that we were able to cut an album called *Keeper of My Heart*.

TRUTH traveled to Cleveland, Tennessee, where we recorded an album at the national headquarters of the Church of God, using their Faith Studios. At that time we weren't under contract with Benson, but we were recording on our own label, Mighty Miracle Music. After we recorded the album, Steve produced it and sold the project to the Benson Company for them to market. That arrangement enabled us to sign a new contract with Benson and make a better financial deal for us.

The Benson people picked up on "Jesus Never Fails" and gave it their best promotion. In June 1981 it became the number one gospel song in America—the first time that had ever happened for TRUTH. The number one song didn't mean that a million people bought the TRUTH record. Disc jockeys around the country voted that song as their first choice for the month. It was nice to pick up the chart and see TRUTH at the top for the first time in ten years.

"Jesus Never Fails" has since become a standard in the industry, known by just about everybody. People love to sing it. I think more for us than anything, the popularity of that one song gave us the right amount of encouragement just at the right time. After all we had gone through in the 1970s, we knew we were no longer on the way back in 1981—we had returned.

In 1976 my mother had died of cancer. Then I lost

my dad. He had suffered from heart attacks from the time I was in elementary school until he died in 1981 of a cancerous brain tumor and heart disease. In 1978 I had been led to face a painful moment of truth about TRUTH. I made the changes, and God's blessings began. Some wouldn't give us a chance to prove ourselves; others didn't seem to want to know anything good about us. But God knew. And God cared.

"Jesus Never Fails" will always be more than just a hit song for me. It will always be a reminder that in fact Jesus never does fail. As I turned TRUTH more surely toward God, God enriched TRUTH's ministry. And I had peace.

JESUS NEVER FAILS*

So many souls have tested Him
Throughout the course of time
So many still reach out to Him
With broken hearts and minds
And everyone of them will say
Without exception that they find
Jesus never fails.

Jesus never fails, Jesus never fails
You might as well get thee behind me Satan
You cannot prevail because
Jesus never fails.

Even in the days of old
He brought His people through
And then He came to show His love
And died for me and you

And then He rose again to prove
That every story had been true
That Jesus never fails.

Sometimes this world brings trouble
I find so hard to bear
I know I could not make it without
Jesus being there
It's so encouraging to know
However deep we're in despair that
Jesus never fails.
So what can I do to prove to you
Tell me how can you deny
No untold facts, no mysteries
It's all so cut and dried
On the witness stand of your life
I'll be the first to testify that
Jesus never fails.

Chapter 7

A Bountiful Moment

"You know my wife and I have loved TRUTH for years," said Stanley King after a concert in Dallas. "We always keep TRUTH people in our homes." This middle-aged man and his wife had become new friends because they loved TRUTH and accepted us so warmly and freely. As Stanley talked, I silently gave thanks to God for people who encourage us as he does. "God has been real good to me, Roger. Real good."

I listened as he told me his story that went something like this: "I'm a geologist. A friend and I went to Midland, Texas, to start drilling for oil. I told the Lord that if he let me hit oil, I'd use the money for Him. The first oil well we sunk was such a gusher that oil ran in the ditches. So now I'm keeping my promise to God.

"Here," he said. He handed me a check for five thousand dollars. I marveled at his generosity so soon after he had bought his local church two buses.

The Kings stayed in touch with us. I had no idea that they would become an ongoing source of encouragement and support for us.

~

While 1981 was a year of miracles and we released "Jesus Never Fails," things were still difficult for us. Maybe that's why we had the miracles—they seem to come when things get pretty bad. And the bad revolved mostly around money.

During the years of trying to change TRUTH, we had built up tremendous debts. The biggest debt was to the Benson Company. In those days, the company functioned like a bank. That is, we bought a lot of record products but paid for only a portion, and they extended credit to us.

We weren't making enough money in the late 1970s to support ourselves, but we did continue to sell records at our concerts. However, instead of using the income to pay the record company, we paid them only a fraction of our sales income and used the rest to keep ourselves alive on the road. Eventually the debt became staggering, and we had to find a way to pay it off.

Linda was doing the books and functioning as our secretary because we were trying not to hire outside help. My brother Billy, who was a career man in the Air Force, was visiting us on leave. When I told him what a hard time we were having, he wanted to help. We suggested he take additional leave so that he could promote a concert or two.

While he was willing to do that, Billy also was annoyed with me. Having been a business major in college, Billy knew how these enterprises worked. Unfortunately I had learned only by doing. He'd tell me what to do to correct something. Mostly he'd start a sentence with, "Roger, didn't you know that . . . ?"

Because I was already out of my element, his suggestions intimidated me, making me feel insecure and inadequate. Things were tough enough for us without having my younger brother tell me how to run my affairs, even though everything he said made sense.

The pressure was building, and every day I worried about owing people. Maybe I really wanted more sympathy and less advice. One day Billy started another of what I called his lectures. Although I could feel the tightening up in my chest and throat, I held myself in check. Finally, unable to listen any more, I looked him right in the eyes and said, "If you know so much about business, why don't you do this for us? Come and join TRUTH."

"Are you kidding? I've got fifteen years in the Air Force," he said. I knew he was thinking that he was only five years away from a full retirement. "You're crazy if you think I'm going to quit the Air Force and come to work for you."

"Fine!" I said, "Then stop telling me how to do it if you're not going to help."

"Fine," Billy snapped back. "Then stop complaining!"

That was mean of me, and I knew it as soon as the words slipped out. But maybe one of the good things about a family is that we can sometimes say words like that, and the relationship continues. Billy turned and walked out of the office. The rest of his time with us, he never said a word about the business end of TRUTH.

I felt bad about the way I had talked to him and yet glad not to have him telling me all the time how foolishly I was handling my affairs. Six months later Billy phoned me and said, "Okay, Roger, I'm on my way."

"What do you mean by 'on your way'?"

"I've decided to leave the Air Force. I'm ready to join TRUTH." By not re-enlisting, my brother Billy gave up every cent of his retirement benefits. He had taken my words seriously. In the days following my blowup, he kept thinking how much we needed his business sense. And he admitted that he had given me a lot of advice, more than I had asked for, and that advice without practical help wasn't very effective. Billy prayed about what to do. Although it was a tough decision, he felt it was time to join TRUTH. I could hardly believe it, but Billy came. He moved to Mobile with his lovely wife, Janet, and son, Brandon. I had not only taught Janet in high school in Opp, but I had introduced her to Billy.

When he got to the office for his first day of work, I had to be out of town, but I wanted him to be an instant part of TRUTH. I bought him a new desk and an executive chair and put them in his office. I also stacked all our bills on top of the desk so he would not have to search for them. On top of the bills I left Billy a note: "Welcome to Mobile. Here it is. Fix it."

I loved dropping all those business details on him

because it took some of the pressure off me. Billy didn't have to tell me the amount of indebtedness because I knew. We owed $439,000. Of that, $105,000 was owed to the Benson Record Company. Almost half a million dollars!

Billy went to work on debt reduction immediately. Within days he had started setting up the system so that we could work out arrangements to pay our debt. Then I received a devastating phone call from Bob McKenzie, president of Benson. "Benson has just been bought out," he said.

While the words sank in, it took me a few seconds to grasp the implications. His next sentence was the real bomb: "I don't want to do this to you, but the new owners are calling in all debts. You owe us $105,000."

"Believe me," I said, "I know exactly how much we owe you." Bob felt terrible for having to lay it on the line—even though I did understand.

"I just don't know how we can raise the money," Billy said. Neither of us realized that the worst was yet to come.

After we discussed the matter for several minutes, Bob McKenzie said, "I have to tell you and I hate like everything to say it, but unless you pay us in ninety days we're going to take the bus." Had it been up to Bob McKenzie, he would have extended our note. This time he had no choice.

After that bomb exploded, nothing Bob said sank in. He was forecasting the end. We owned a 1974 bus, and we *needed* it. Without it we couldn't travel and earn more money. Billy and I talked over the situation. Neither of us knew what to do. I couldn't go to the bank and borrow even a hundred thousand dollars. Not with the debts we owed.

Right at that crisis point, we were ready for our scheduled ten-year reunion. When the former members of TRUTH were all together I said, "You know what, gang? I want us to enjoy this weekend because there may never be another one. I don't know what's going to happen to TRUTH." They expressed their concern. Despite the dark clouds we had a wonderful reunion with over two hundred people present, including families of our alumni.

On July 9, a week after the reunion, Billy went with me to Bedford, Texas, where TRUTH was giving a concert in a football stadium. We had until August 15 to pay Benson. Among several people I trusted, I had talked with Stanley King on the phone about the phenomenal debt we faced. I didn't ask him for money, and he didn't offer any. "My family and I will be at the Bedford concert," he said. At the stadium TRUTH was to one side near the middle of the field. Between us and the small audience were a fence and a track. Anybody who wanted to make a decision for Jesus Christ and come forward would have had to walk down to the goal posts to get there. It just didn't work. The love offering was $750.

The recent loss of my dad was already weighing heavily on me. With the low evening and our rising debts, I was sad and discouraged. Understandably, my discouragement showed when after the meeting several of us were having something to eat. Among those eating with us was our friend from Houston, Stanley King. As we talked, the matter of our huge debt came up. Then Stanley asked, "What are you going to do about the Benson bill?"

"I don't know," I said.

"I honestly don't know. I guess they have a bus because I don't have the money to pay it."

Without another word, Stanley reached into his pocket and pulled out a check. He handed it to me. I stared at the amount. Tears clouded my eyes, but I finally read aloud the figure he had written—$105,000.

Kim Noblitt, then our road director, was sitting at another table with his mother. I was so excited that I rushed over, waving the check. "We got it! We got it!" I said.

The next day Billy and I flew to Nashville and paid off the Benson Company—in full.

That payment didn't erase our financial problems, however. We were still in debt over $250,000. While we still had our bus, it was falling apart, in need of major repairs. Our sound equipment was outdated; we needed new clothes for members of TRUTH. By the end of the month, I knew we wouldn't be able to pay salaries and current bills. Even so, I was encouraged.

The next gift came from a totally unexpected and not altogether welcome source. All through the years Linda had been so supportive, so uncomplaining, that I had wanted to do something really special for her. In 1980 I had bought beautiful Omega watches for us. Linda was a little nervous about wearing hers because it was a blue lapis lazuli bracelet watch with diamonds all over it.

One day during the period of heavy financial

strain, Linda said, "Roger, TRUTH is hurting so desperately. I have this beautiful watch, but I can't wear it when I think of how bad things are. Sell my watch. . . . I'll never wear this watch again."

My feelings were hurt because I'd bought the watch for her. But I agreed. It took three months before we sold both watches, but we did, and we gave the money to the Lord. I bought myself a nineteen-dollar Timex in Evansville, Indiana. At first my pride was wounded a little. I was still a bit of a strutter at the time, perhaps making up for what I didn't have during my growing-up years.

I was learning that possessions aren't really that important. But I'm slow at learning and God worked patiently with me. One of the toughest lessons for me was that God wanted to change me before changing my circumstances. Someone shared with me four ways God answers prayer. I would live long enough to experience all four: 1) No, not yet. 2) No, I love you too much. 3) Yes, I thought you'd never ask. 4) Yes, and here's more. Then, after a concert in late January 1981, a man said, "Roger, I've got something I'd like to give you. It's in my pocket right now." "Sure," I said, thinking that he had a check to help us with our heavy debt.

He was embarrassed and said, "It's seven years old, and if you won't be offended, I'd like to give it to you."

"I promise I won't be offended."

From his pocket he pulled out a watch. "My wife gave me a new one for Christmas. And, well, I thought . . . I thought you might like this. If you don't want to wear it, you're free to sell it. I just wanted to do something for you." It was a Rolex—the kind of watch I had never expected to own or had even thought of having. "You need to have it appraised," he said.

I had it appraised at $4,500—worth far more than the watch I had bought—and sold. I was so thankful to God. Specifically I recall praying, "Lord Jesus, I've never given You anything that You didn't give back better. Even though I never expected to have a Rolex watch, You gave me one. Thank you, God, for teaching me such a valuable lesson."

But I hadn't fully learned. Not yet.

~

Three months later Linda and I were in San Francisco, and Billy phoned us with bad news. There had been a lot of bad news during that first year he worked for TRUTH. "We don't have enough money to pay salaries."

By this time I had sold everything I had, including one of my cars. "I don't have anything else to sell," I said. "We haven't taken in much so far on the road. All I've got is the Thunderbird, and I don't want to sell that." The Thunderbird was my dream car and had been paid off for only four months.

Linda, who heard my end of the conversation, said, "Roger, God probably isn't going to use you until you are willing to give up everything for Him."

"Everything? Haven't I given up everything?"

"Have you?"

"Linda, you know I have." But as I said the words I

knew what she was thinking. I had only one thing left . . . and I didn't want to part with my 1957 two-seater Thunderbird. Some boys grow up wanting to own a Cadillac or an Alfa Romeo. Ever since my junior high days when a classmate rode to school in a 1957 T-Bird, my one dream had been to own one just like it. I finally found just the one I wanted, already a collector's item. After negotiating a good price of $10,500, I made monthly payments for three years and had only recently paid it off.

What I said to Linda was, "I've told God that everything I have is His, and I've given God everything."

"All right, Roger," she said, "if you say so." I didn't want Linda to say anything more because deep inside I knew she was right.

Linda's spiritual devotion has always been amazing to me. She lives out daily her feeling that we must never clutch God's gifts selfishly nor forget where they have come from. Her example is a tough one to follow, but I have always found myself enriched by God's blessing when I do follow.

As I thought about our situation, I remembered an incident that had happened two months earlier at a service in Huntsville, Alabama. The pastor preached about tithing and their need for a new building. We had come to sing especially to boost the presentation for the church's building program.

As usually happens, they didn't take a love offering for us until the end of the concert. While the pastor was preaching, the Lord spoke to me: Whatever the love offering amounted to, I was to give it back to the church for the building program. At first, the thought overwhelmed me, and silently I argued with God, reminding Him of our pressing need.

But the persistent inner voice wouldn't quit, so I said "Okay, God—because You say so."

God also told me something else that night. The words were so clear in my heart—sell the Thunderbird to help pay TRUTH's debts. I was so overcome with the matter of returning the offering, I didn't give much thought to the T-Bird. Or perhaps I intentionally didn't want to think about that part of what God had told me.

At the end of the service, I said, "I'm returning this offering to you, pastor. Not because we don't need it but because I want to obey God who told me to do this." The people were touched and excited, and it felt good for us to give help toward a church's building program.

I gave the money back, but I didn't say a word about the Thunderbird to anybody. Since that concert, the matter of the Thunderbird had haunted me. While definitely a luxury, it was the one thing I'd always wanted to own, and I had waited twenty-five years. What I hadn't realized, Linda had been praying specifically about the Thunderbird but never spoke about it to me.

Then Billy's call came, and when I said all I had was a Thunderbird, I remembered that the Lord had spoken to me a few weeks before about the car. Linda's comments after the conversation only added to the pressure. I couldn't run away any longer.

"Okay, God," I said.

I called Billy back. "Sell the Thunderbird."

"You're sure?" he asked. He knew how strongly attached I felt to the car.

"Yes," I said.

"And, Billy, I don't want to see it when I come back. Whether you sell it or not, make sure it's not there when we get back. Okay?" I was so heavy-hearted, I didn't want to think about the car again. At the same time, I sensed that God was lovingly and tenderly (but not without my feeling a lot of pain) teaching me that I must not hold back anything. Billy called the man I bought the T-Bird from and asked, "How much do you think we could get for it?"

"If you can sell it for $15,000," he said, "you'd better take it."

"I'm going to get $17,000," Billy said with determination in his voice. Billy phoned a man in Texas and offered it to him. "We need to sell this car because we're hurting financially."

"How much?"

"We'd like $20,000," Billy said, figuring he'd probably have to come down. He described the car.

"If you'll deliver it tomorrow, I'll give you the $20,000."

"It'll be there."

Billy called me back that night and told me. While I was happy for the $20,000, I was just sick about losing my T-Bird. I couldn't go to that night's concert in Petaluma, California, because I wasn't feeling well. The hurt and the disappointment inside had really thrown me. So I stayed in the motel all evening, trying to pray, wanting victory over this grief but unable to gain it.

I had given up the last thing I had, the only thing I'd ever wanted. Although the Bible speaks about giving joyfully and cheerfully, I hadn't reached that point. "Oh, God," I moaned. "You know I haven't asked for much for myself. But now you strip even this away." I was feeling sorry for myself and really miserable.

That same night Billy called again. He had talked to the man in Texas. "Roger, the man just called and said he wouldn't give us the $20,000 for the car."

"He's backed out?" Momentarily I thought that maybe God had only been testing me and that I'd have the car back.

"Not exactly," Billy said and laughed. "He wanted to know what we'd use the money for. When I told him for the ministry of TRUTH, he said, 'If you can deliver it tomorrow, I'll give you $50,000 for it.'"

"Sell it!" I said, and a new sense of joy and peace overwhelmed me. "Thanks, God," I said. In my hands, the car was worth $10,000—what I paid for it. When I gave it to God, he multiplied it by five for the kingdom of God.

"God is really good," I said to Linda.

On August 2, 1981, on our way back from California, we stopped in Las Vegas for a concert. To my surprise a wonderful couple, Tommy and Patty Hyde, whom I hadn't seen in months, showed up. They had come to Las Vegas so that he could play in an important golf tournament. He invited me to join them for breakfast the next morning. "I know TRUTH has had a lot of money troubles," he said. "Are things getting any better?"

"You wouldn't believe how much better," I said

and laughed. "Or maybe you would. God has touched the hearts of several people who have been able to give us substantial amounts." For a few minutes I shared highlights of the first seven months of the year. We had a few tears and a lot of smiles on our faces. Then I read to them Psalm 119:71–72. Ever since the sale of the T-Bird, those two verses had become God's word of guidance for me:

> It is good for me that I have been afflicted,
> That I may learn Your statutes.
> The law of Your mouth is better to me
> Than thousands of shekels of gold and silver.

During the conversation the matter of the bus came up. "It's been a great bus," I said, "but we've already put a million miles on it; it's ready for retirement. And as soon as the Lord sees fit, we'll get a new one."

We talked about other things and then parted from each other.

"We're praying for you," Tommy said as we parted.

On August 10 I received a lengthy letter from Tommy in which he said, "God spoke to me during our breakfast meeting." He was on the verge of selling his company, and if it came about, his letter said, "I will invest a substantial amount of money toward a new bus for TRUTH. Or you can use it for major repairs on your present bus."

On December 22 we needed $13,000 to meet our current bills prior to taking our Christmas break. As I did regularly, I called a friend in Florida to give him an update on what God was doing in our year of miracles. I mentioned the immediate problem. He listened and rejoiced with me. When I hung up, I felt at peace, knowing that somehow God would come through. And God did. The next day, our Florida friend wired us $15,000. And the year wasn't over.

On December 26, Tommy Hyde called. "Roger, the sale is going through this week." We rejoiced together, and he closed by saying, "I've not forgotten my promise." He didn't forget. On December 29, he wired $97,000 to our bank in Mobile. We couldn't buy a new bus for that amount, but we did the next best thing: we completely overhauled our old one. And it was like having a new bus.

In January of 1981 we had started out at an all-time low with no cash and a half-million-dollar debt. Not only did the amount stagger me, but I hadn't been able to see any way to pay it off. By December 31, 1981, we had cut that figure in half. God had used obedient individuals to work miracle after miracle in the ministry of TRUTH. I felt so privileged that God had called me to be one of them. The watch and the Thunderbird have paled in my memory while the recollection of TRUTH's survival and victory in Christ remain a miraculous source of hope for me today. We were living in Ephesians 3:20: "Now to Him who is able to do exceeding abundantly beyond all that we ask or think, according to the power that works within us."

We still weren't out of debt, but we were on the way. We had thrown off the heavy load and could concentrate more fully on serving Jesus Christ.

And in the process, I learned so much.

Chapter 8

A Miraculous Moment

TRUTH was moving along the road to financial recovery. We still had ups and downs, but we kept going. Some days I wondered how we'd make it, but God faithfully provided. In 1985 we were almost out of debt.

Then another blow fell. "We've had the bus for twelve years," I said to Linda, "and it's as tired as I am."

The bus, customized for us when we bought it new, had given us a lot of good service. We had been able to overhaul it five years earlier, but now it was really showing its age. It was no longer dependable.

"I know," she answered, "and it was a miracle that we could buy that one. Maybe God will help us with another miracle."

"Not just another miracle—a bigger one."

For twelve years that bus had been on the road approximately 330 days and 99,000 miles annually. That's a lot of miles.

"We'll just have to keep on praying," my wife said. She knew that I had been praying for a couple of years for God to give us a new bus. Since no bus had appeared, we would just keep on.

I had no idea of the current price of specialized vehicles. We had paid $120,000 in 1974, and customized vehicles had obviously gone up considerably in those years. We had been doing so well that I had projected replacing the bus by the mid-eighties.

Then we hit a snag—something I couldn't explain except to say that we had leveled out. Financially we weren't progressing, and our annual income had stayed the same for five years. My boys were getting older and the expenses were higher, yet I hadn't had a raise for five years.

I prayed; Linda prayed; members of TRUTH and a few select friends prayed. Nothing happened. Even so, I felt we needed a new bus, not only larger but with a differently designed interior. This time we needed a sleeper bus big enough for most of our twenty people to sleep in because we were often driving overnight to get to our concerts.

Then came Christmas, and the year was almost over. Christmas of 1985 was a significant one in my life because I thought of the years I had been on the road. Although we had no surplus funds, we had paid our debts. I wished we had enough to give well-deserved bonuses, especially to the office staff.

As Christmas came around, I felt myself sinking lower and lower. *Why am I doing this anyway? Is it time to stop traveling and settle down with a dependable job?* I kept thinking of the bus. We had begun to have one kind of mechanical problem after another, and that frustrated me.

Along with that problem, my close friends were saying, "Roger, God has been good to you. You've had a great ministry, but now your family is growing up. Isn't it time for you to settle down and come home?" Other friends said, "It's time for God to give you a new ministry."

Of course I listened; they were my friends. The more I thought of what they kept telling me, the more I started to believe them. *It's over,* I recall saying to myself. *It's over.*

When we broke for the Christmas holidays, I didn't know if I wanted to start TRUTH again in 1986. "God, I'm going home to Mobile, and I'm turning in my keys to you. I'm tired. I'm finished." Fifteen years on the road, and I had finally decided it was enough.

"Lord," I said, "you can have this job. I can't take it anymore." I was prepared to call all the members of TRUTH during the Christmas break and say, "I can't furnish the accommodations you need like updated equipment and a new bus. Don't come back. I'm going to do something else to earn a living. This is just too hard."

I probably rehearsed my little speech forty times, trying to say it right. But in effect, I wanted to say to the kids, "I can't get us a new bus. I can't make it happen anymore so I'm quitting."

Three days before the members of TRUTH were

scheduled to return, the doorbell awakened me at seven-thirty in the morning. Linda and the boys were asleep. And being a musician with a lot of late hours, I don't get up early. For a few seconds I thought maybe the offending person at my door would go away. The bell rang again. Finally I pulled myself out of bed and went downstairs to the door.

A man named Mike Bodenhamer was standing in front of me, wearing a brown suit and a sharp tie. I knew Mike, but he'd never been to my house before and my foggy brain couldn't figure out why he'd chosen this time to come. "Roger, God sent me here to tell you something."

Mike's a nice fellow; under normal circumstances I would have been delighted to see him. At seven-thirty in the morning, however, I forced a smile, opened the door, and said, "Sure, come on inside," while I mumbled under my breath, "I don't need this kind of hassle." It was early, and I was still pretty discouraged.

"Roger, do you have a Bible?" he asked as soon as he walked past me.

"I'm sure we have one around here someplace," I said, trying to make a joke of it. He followed me into my study and I handed him a Bible. He sat down, started to open the Bible, and then shook his head. He handed it to me.

"You do it, Roger. I want you to read Habakkuk 2:3 out loud." I took the Bible, my mood even worse than when the doorbell awakened me. I was beginning to suspect that this ordinarily nice fellow had come to give me some heavy Bible verse to heap a million pounds of guilt on top of me.

As I opened the Bible, I paused before I read it and looked at Mike. "Habakkuk 2:3?" He nodded and tears rolled down his face. I read:

> For the vision is yet for an appointed time;
> But at the end it will speak, and it will not lie.
> Though it tarries, wait for it;
> Because it will surely come,
> It will not tarry.

A strange feeling came over the room, and I stared at him, not knowing what to say or how to react. Finally Mike stopped crying, got up, and said, "I feel I need to pray for you and TRUTH and all the people who come to the concerts." He started praying right then.

The best way I know to describe what happened is to say that as the words came out of his mouth, the glory of the Lord filled my study. I had a sense of how Moses must have felt when God told him to take off his shoes because he stood on holy ground. While I didn't cry, I felt humbled and ashamed for doubting God's will. I felt an overwhelming rush of gratitude as I realized that God had sent someone to speak to me in my moment of need.

As soon as he finished praying, Mike said, "Roger, that's what God told me to tell you. I have to go now, or I'll be late for work." He walked out of the house. As he left, I couldn't think of anything but that verse:

> For the vision is yet for an appointed time;
> But at the end it will speak. . . .
> Though it tarries, wait for it. . . .

"It has tarried all right," I said, and now I knew God was encouraging me and telling me not to put an end to TRUTH.

When Linda came downstairs, I told her what happened, and she felt encouraged too. She squeezed my hand. "Then we wait." For the first time in weeks, I felt totally at peace. Even though I still had no idea what was going to happen, something was on the way. I was willing to wait.

Mike had been so interested in our ministry, it had seemed natural to confide in him. He knew about our need for a new bus, and I had previously asked him to pray about the need with us. However, he didn't know that I was disillusioned and planning to quit.

On January 16, 1986, the members of TRUTH came back. We started rehearsing for our next year on the road. In the middle of the morning I received a telephone call from George Sanders in Florida. "I know you need a bus. I'm calling because I want to help you buy it. How much will it cost?" I knew exactly what he meant: He was going to give us a large sum of money to help buy the bus.

By then I had calculated that a new bus would cost just about the amount of the half-million-dollar debt that TRUTH had just paid off. By 1986 an empty bus with just a driver's seat and a steering wheel cost about $170,000. A bus with the features we needed would cost about $375,000.

When I told him, he said, "I'll pay for the shell of the bus. It's up to you to raise the rest of the money." The rest of the money was another quarter of a million dollars.

This was the same man who had given TRUTH so much back in 1981, beginning with $2,500 in the offering and then $10,000 and $50,000 on top of that. Mike had wept in my study. Now tears filled my eyes. I prayed; I sang; I thanked God; I called Linda and felt as if, like David of old, I could have danced before God. Anybody who knows me realizes I can't dance, but I sure felt like it.

"We got a bus! We got a bus!"

In reality, we didn't have a bus—not yet, but I knew it would happen. Billy and I began negotiating to buy a bus. Because vehicles of this type are customized, it takes four or five months to get one after the order is placed. We had to decide where to buy it and who would do the interior—which was absolutely critical because of our special needs. We wanted a bus to sleep at least sixteen, one that had three state rooms, a microwave oven and a refrigerator, two tables, and good restroom facilities.

As Billy and I moved forward in negotiating, I had to raise enough money to pay for the interior. Everyone who knew the business about customized buses said that the folks in Columbus, Ohio, were the finest bus conversion people in America. I made several trips to their factory, and everything I saw was just right. We found the bus we wanted, and we found the company to do the interior. They told us, "You can expect delivery by the end of June."

The message from Habakkuk recharged my own batteries. We had a great selection of music to offer, and the kids were as excited as any group I've ever had. And I had committed TRUTH to $375,000 for the bus. We received some gifts during the next few months but nothing large and not nearly enough when it was all added up.

The company informed me that, with cash in hand, I could pick up the bus on June 27, 1986. Mr Sanders followed through on his pledge. We also got help from the John Price Foundation in Ft. Myers, Florida. John Price was the older man who years earlier had given me $2,500 at the same time that George Sanders had given me that amount. By this time John Price had passed away, but the trustee-administrator, Wayne Miller, wanted to help us as well.

Money was coming in, just not fast enough. To make it easier for us, we scheduled a concert in Columbus, Ohio, for the night of June 27. Unfortunately, we still didn't have enough money that night to make one final payment on the bus. In the account marked bus, we were still short $107,000.

Officials from the bus company picked me up at the airport at ten o'clock that morning and drove me to their factory. Quite proudly they showed me the bus, completely finished, parked in front, just waiting for me to drive it away. They had received $268,000 in payments, and now we had reached the last hour. For days I'd been praying fervently for the remaining amount, and it hadn't come. *What am I going to do, God? What am I going to do?* I prayed.

No great words of wisdom came to me. After the president gave me a tour of the bus, we headed toward his office for the final payment. On the way I said, "Man, I don't know what to tell you. I just don't have the money."

"I'll tell you one thing, Roger," he said calmly.

"The bus isn't going to leave our parking lot until we get every dime."

"I understand your position," I said. "I'm just not sure what to do now."

"Let's have lunch," he said, "and maybe by then you can figure out how to get the rest of the money."

"Sure," I said. I went back out to the bus again, just to gaze at it by myself. *Oh, God,* I pleaded once I was alone, *you said it would happen. That even if it tarried, I was to wait. I don't see how I can wait much longer.*

We had lunch, and then I said, "Give me an office where I can sit down and make a few telephone calls. That's all I can think of right now." I called Billy and asked him to make calls. Both Billy and I talked to every banker we knew.

More than an hour after I began making calls, I still hadn't come up with the rest of the money. Even if we raised it that afternoon, at that point I didn't know if it would do any good. They demanded a cashier's check. I was at a loss. Mentally I quoted Habakkuk again, but no miracle exploded before my eyes.

I recalled that as I left home that morning, Linda had said, "Roger, read 2 Chronicles 20:15b." I had read it, underlined it and had then forgotten the verse. At one-fourteen, beginning to feel a little discouraged, I opened my Bible and read it again: "Do not be afraid nor dismayed because of this great multitude, for the battle is not yours, but Gods."

At two o'clock I was still making telephone calls.

Finally I called Mr. Sanders. He knew the president of the bus company. Mr. Sanders asked me to get the president on the line. After a lengthy discussion with the president and with me, Mr. Sanders said, "Well, Roger, I think we've worked out a couple of snags."

Mr. Sanders had come through again. He wired money from Florida to Columbus, Ohio. Just after four-thirty I was driving that beautiful new bus out of the parking lot, and I reached the church by five o'clock. As I pulled up in the church lot, I was emotionally and physically weak. Five hours earlier I had needed more than $100,000 and had no idea where it would possibly come from. By five o'clock I was riding to the church to meet TRUTH in this brand new customized bus. The gifts that day were miraculous beyond anyone's expectation. They had come from our friends at Mark III Vans and Norman Archibald. Mr. Sanders loaned us the remainder. After several payments, he forgave the balance.

The members of TRUTH literally surrounded the bus in the parking lot and praised God for it. But perhaps the highest moment of all was my opportunity at the concert that night to share the miracle that God had wrought through obedient servants.

That's not quite the end of the story of our bus. A fellow named Johnny Williams, who loves TRUTH and is my friend, lives in Montgomery, Alabama. Johnny used to work on buses, so he often helped us repair and fix up the 1974 bus.

"Roger, I'd love to buy this old TRUTH bus one day," he said.

I grinned. "I'd love to sell it to you, and we desperately need a new bus. I'll tell you what. If God gives me a new bus, I'll sell you this old one." I had named a price like $50,000 to $60,000, not having any idea of its value (later I learned it was worth more like $80,000 to $90,000).

When Mr. Sanders gave us the new bus, I called Johnny Williams. "I told you I'd sell you this bus if we got a new one. Mr. Sanders is going to help us get a new one." I'd been praying about this for several days, and so I said, "But I don't feel like I can sell it to you. What I'm going to do is I'm going to give it to you."

He was, of course, overwhelmed and deeply touched. And I felt good because I truly believed God had spoken to me to do that. I was so humbled by the fact that God would use people like Mr. Sanders and others to bless us the way he did, I had to give away the 1974 bus. God had given us a miraculous gift, and TRUTH's gift to Johnny was a small way to respond to His lovingkindness.

God had taught us so much. As we had received so abundantly, we had also learned to give. We even learned to give out of our own need—beyond our ability (2 Corinthians 8:2, 3). I've never regretted giving that bus to Johnny. Already I'm hoping that one day we can give our 1986 bus away too and that we won't have to wait twelve years to do it.

As a footnote, in the 1988 presidential campaign, Pat Robertson toured in our old bus, now called *Asphalt I* until he lost the Republican nomination. Afterward, George Bush used it while he was touring across the United States. Johnny Williams drove it during the entire campaign. It has become the most photographed bus in the world.

A couple of my friends teased me over that one.

"The 1974 bus wasn't good enough for you, but it was good enough for the president of the United States."

This one miracle stands out in my mind profoundly as another instance of God's teaching me how to wait for His appointed time. And as my patience grows, so does my internal peace.

Chapter 9

A Moment of Vision

For as long as I can remember, I've had a sense of mission beyond the United States. While we gave money for foreign work and we prayed for those on the front lines, I sensed that God wanted me to do something more. After our Tijuana, Mexico, concert in 1976, I knew that TRUTH had to continue ministering beyond the bounds of the continental United States. It just seemed like the right thing to do.

I was excited as the invitations abroad began to come in. Linda and the boys were excited too. After Linda accepted my being on the road in 1971, she wholeheartedly supported TRUTH's expansion into new areas. TRUTH has always been in her prayers, and now those prayers have followed us halfway around the world.

If it hadn't been for the trust that Linda and I have built and strengthened over the years, I could never have gone on tour to another continent, leaving her and the boys behind. I knew that however far away I was physically, Linda would be showing and teaching our boys what they needed to know to grow up in the Lord.

Our relationship has deepened so profoundly over our years on the road that, no matter how much I missed my family, I didn't have to worry about what was going on at home. Linda has always been open with me about what went on in my absence. I always knew every detail and had an opportunity to be involved in decisions.

With Linda and her prayers behind me and three fine sons watching their father's life in the ministry, how could I not follow God's call to foreign lands?

We made a whirlwind blitz of Europe in 1977. Linda was able to join us for this tour. In seventeen days, we put on twenty-seven concerts in Luxembourg, Germany, Holland, and Sweden. One of the highlights was at the De Doelen Hall in Rotterdam, Holland, one of the most beautiful concert halls in the world. We were guest artists along with the Young Credo Singers, a choir of about 150 very professional, well-trained singers.

As part of this trip we worked with Bob McKenzie, who was making a film on the life of John Wesley. During our blitz we also recorded a live album and taped a television special. I had anticipated a time of relaxation during this first overseas tour. It turned out that by the time we returned to Mobile, we were exhausted and needed a rest. Even so, we loved the tour.

But Europe was not the only foreign territory where God was planning to use TRUTH. Over the years we have been given a chance to grow and serve in places that made the little church with the outdoor restroom facilities look like a palace.

A few months after the European tour, we made a wonderful trip to Jamaica. My friend, Mr. Soulhail Karram, sponsored us in the eight-day tour. Although born in Lebanon, he grew up and has lived in Jamaica most of his life. Soulhail Karram is a remarkable Christian who arranged for us to do concerts in Kingston, Mandeville, and Montego Bay.

The music attracted thousands of people and was a fantastic experience for us. One of the more meaningful concerts took place on the lawn of the deputy prime minister's home in Kingston. That night Communists stopped the buses to prevent people from coming to the concert. Only those who walked were able to attend, and we had a poor showing—only three to four thousand people! (Otherwise we would have had at least twice that number.) No matter how long I live, I'll never forget the sight and sound of those people singing "How Great Thou Art." It was a special moment for me.

All through the late seventies and early eighties, the years of crisis and change for TRUTH, those mission experiences lingered in my memory. Habakkuk's message about waiting for the "appointed" time had significance for more than our need for a new bus. I had to wait to continue a foreign ministry as well. As God brought our ministry out of debt and provided us with a means of transportation, I knew that He was affirming my vision of service in foreign nations.

All this time Linda was with me in looking toward

the future. She continued to pray and yearn for the changes in our lives that would bring TRUTH into the foreign mission field again. She has for some time believed that it is God's intention to use TRUTH in the last days' revival around the world. And indeed God has already begun doing that in ways that we never imagined or dreamed in the early eighties.

In 1985 we went to Brazil under the sponsorship of Nilson Fanini, whom many people call the Billy Graham of South America. He's the pastor of First Baptist Church in Niteroi, Brazil. Bob Hobbs of World Vision, who later founded an organization dedicated to helping the poor in the third world, worked it out for us to go to Brazil to observe Fanini's ministry. An interesting note, this invitation from Bob came the same week in January as my visit from Mike Bodenhamer and the call about our new bus.

After seeing Fanini at work and observing first-hand his deep sense of compassion, I suspect he could be the next president of Brazil because he has so much influence in the country. Fanini is a godly man with a degree in law and a doctoral degree in theology. He sets aside every Tuesday afternoon for the Brazilians who line up to seek his advice. He is their spiritual father, their counselor, and their lawyer. He starts at noon, and he stays until the last one leaves, usually about dark.

Fanini is somewhere between his mid-forties and his early fifties, a handsome man with a kind spirit. He is distinguished looking, just under six feet tall, and slender. Although he can be eloquent enough in his speech to be intimidating, he's such a gentle man. His presence is commanding when he walks into a room, and he knows how to listen when people talk.

At our first meeting, I sensed immediately that he is concerned about everything, not just problems in Brazil, but concerns around the whole world.

And what a preacher! One night Fanini spoke in the stadium at Rio, and over 200,000 people attended with 40,000 people making decisions.

On another occasion Fanini had an appointment with the president of Brazil. He planned to ask for the use of their television network. Like Nehemiah, the king's cupbearer (see Neh. 1:11), he prayed that God would grant him favor. Several of the large industries in Brazil wanted to buy the television station, but Fanini wanted it to be used primarily to send out the gospel.

Fanini walked into the president of Brazil's office, and before he could speak a word the president said, "I want to give you the network. It is yours. You may have it."

From CBN, Pat Robertson gave Fanini more than fifty thousand dollars for his ministry one year. He assumed that Fanini would use the gift as seed money in raising other funds in the States. Instead, as Robertson found out, Fanini took every cent back home and placed it where it would most benefit the poor. The next year Pat Robertson gave him a TV tower, worth several hundred thousand dollars.

I had already been impressed by what I had heard about Fanini before I went to Brazil, but actually seeing his ministry in the slums touched me deeply. We stayed in the homes of local people, a real eye-opener for us. It was incredible to see what this one man has done in these mountainous barrios where the people

live. In parts of the region, they have so much violence, the police won't go near them. But Fanini
does.

We followed him around, visited the shacks, and
prayed with the people. Many of them don't have
bathrooms, running water, electricity, or any of the
conveniences we expect in our country. Two of our
guys found a grandmother lying on a foam mattress.
She was eighty years old and dying. Her pain was
so severe she was almost out of her mind, and she
lay there, chewing on the foam rubber. They had a
chance to pray for her, and her pain eased.

We sang on the landing site of the *Barcas*—a ferry-
boat that hundreds of people ride between Rio and
Niteroi. As soon as we started, people flocked to listen. In two nights of ministry, we saw almost seven
hundred people saved. It was a great eye-opener for
us to experience South America and to grasp the
number of hurting people of the third world.

But I especially want to share an experience that
occurred only hours after our arrival in Brazil. The
church people took us to the slums immediately.
Most of the huts were little more than some kind of
protection from the rain. Road signs and large pieces
of cardboard often provided the only protection they
had against the elements. The smell of open sewers
was everywhere.

In the first mud hut I walked into, I saw a woman
and three boys. The hut had two tiny rooms with one
small cot on the floor. Although the mother looked
about fourteen, she was probably closer to forty. The
Brazilian pastor with us said to me, "I want you to
share Jesus with this lady."

I was a little nervous, and I didn't know the language (he interpreted), so I started speaking. She sat quietly, staring at me, her eyes never leaving my face. When I finished, she nodded to the interpreter and began to rattle in Portuguese. The pastor interpreted her words. "Tell that American I don't want his Jesus and I don't need his Jesus. I've got three sons here, and we haven't eaten in three days. If he's interested in helping me, tell that American he can give me money. We don't have anything to eat."

That was my introduction to Brazil.

I couldn't think of anything appropriate to say. Saying I'm sorry wouldn't have been enough. Speechless, I turned and walked out. We had been instructed not to give money because it encourages begging, especially from North Americans like us. With the church people being there and obviously hearing her, the church people got food to her—they are just that kind of people. Even so, I felt overwhelmed by the experience. Right then I made up my mind that when we got back to the States, we were going to help the work of the church in the third world. We would raise funds to do what we could. *A million dollars,* I kept thinking. *We need to raise a million dollars.*

We stayed in Niteroi for ten days singing concerts, observing the ministry, and rejoicing as many made decisions for Christ. By the time we returned to America, I had caught the fever for missions: I wanted every Christian in America to catch the same vision.

Using a multimedia presentation, we toured the country sharing our Brazil experiences with our audiences. My vision was that after deducting our expenses, we would send the rest of the offerings to Brazil. We raised $200,000 for that ministry. That amount was nowhere near the million dollars I had wanted to raise—but it was a start.

The focus of our ministry had now changed. God had placed in my heart a vision for the hurting world. It's hard to describe it to overfed, middle-class Americans, but Linda and I are prepared to do whatever we can to work for and help hungry and hurting people in any way we can, spiritually and physically. As I urge people to open themselves to the need of others, I wonder if people get tired of hearing about needs in the third world. Yet I can't forget the overwhelming experience of boarding a plane in Miami and then, only hours later, stepping into a mud hut.

The experience with the woman still haunts me. I can hear her voice and feel the anger spewing from her. I'm thankful that God has used Fanini's ministry to ease her pain and bring her hope.

~

As I flew back to Miami I recall thinking, *Welcome to the third world, Roger—the world of painful reality*. I had suffered moments of fear about finances, moments of worry about how my vision for this ministry would affect those around me. But I had never suffered as deeply as these people I was leaving behind me in Brazil. And I was more determined than ever to be part of the solution.

Chapter 10

A Moment of Mission

"I'd like to tell you a story," the man said on the telephone in early 1988. He gave his name, but I caught only the first one, David.

"Sure, tell me," I said.

He was paying for the call, and I had a sense that it was important. "On July 29, 1975, I was a high school student and I went to a TRUTH concert at the First United Methodist Church in Fairhope, Alabama. Because I got there late, I had to stand in the back. The place was packed. At the conclusion of the concert, you gave an altar call. I responded, and that night I gave my heart to Jesus Christ.

"You see, Roger," he said, "I didn't come from a strong Christian family. Maybe that was part of the trouble. My parents were divorced. I rebelled and didn't want anything to do with Jesus Christ. Before that night, I had rebelled in every way I knew how. I had also been arrested seven times. Finally I was tired of running from God. When Art Ortiz sang 'The Lord Is My Light,' something happened inside of me; I stopped running. After I became a Christian, I felt God calling me into the ministry, so I went to Bible college." He explained that after college, he became an evangelist and traveled across the United States, Canada, and the Orient. In Canada David met a lovely young woman named Bev and married her.

"I haven't seen TRUTH in twelve years, but I've kept up with your ministry," he said. "My dad still lives in Fairhope, Alabama, and he sends me your tapes. Even though I haven't heard from you directly, I feel a special place in my heart for the ministry of TRUTH.

"I'm now a pastor, and I've been praying for days about making this phone call. So the purpose of my call is to ask if you'd come and sing in my church?"

I was thinking, after an introduction like that, how could I turn him down? "If you come, you'll get to sing in my new building. We're putting the roof on right now. It seats ten thousand."

"Ten thousand?" That figure overwhelmed me. It also confused me because only a handful of American churches are that large. I thought I knew all the megachurches, and I couldn't link him with any of them. "Where is your church?"

"In Manila. The Philippines." That really startled me, and my enthusiasm shrank. "Right now, I just don't know. But I'll sure pray about it and get back with you."

The more I prayed about TRUTH going to Manila, the more convinced I became that God wanted us to minister there. We were just starting out on the road again after the Christmas holidays. I thought that if we had a good year we could go just after Christmas.

In 1988 we did 309 concerts. We raised $91,000— which is what we needed for twenty-five of us to make the trip with all of our equipment and to be able to stay and minister for over two weeks. On January 18, 1989, we left from Dallas, and after intermediate stops we landed in Manila.

By now I knew the young pastor's name was David Sumrall. He is what I call a theological intellectual— meaning he's a sharp fellow, who understands not only how to do things but why. David and Bev have been in the Philippines since 1980. Bev is the minister of music at the church, and they also have a Bible college. David's one of the bright young men internationally today, and I'm thrilled that TRUTH played a small role in introducing him to Christ.

When David told me they were completing the building and putting the roof on it, I envisioned the stone or brick buildings we normally see in the States. This building wasn't quite that way. The best way to describe the church is to say that when a new sanctuary in America is 50 percent complete, it is 100 percent complete in the Philippines. The church, Cathedral of Praise, does seat ten thousand; it is located on a side street, behind an old tin fence. Despite what looks rough and unfinished to us, to them it is a grand building.

We spent seventeen days in the Philippines, giving thirty-seven concerts to about a quarter of a million people. During those concerts approximately twenty thousand people accepted Jesus Christ as Savior—one of the most encouraging and meaningful things that has ever happened in our ministry.

We didn't try to tour the 7,500 islands of the Philippines but stayed in Manila, which is like a country itself. Besides the concerts, we helped in street ministry, and we sang in many of the schools and universities. We participated in the most organized endeavor we've ever been involved in.

One thing that happened with David Sumrall that has never happened with us before was the remarkable follow-up system. David had nine computers going twenty-four hours a day with two thousand volunteers doing follow-up. Workers took the names of all those who made decisions at any of the locations. All names went into a computer listing, and then they put the new converts under the supervision of team captains. Every new person got visited at least five times.

Eighty people comprise the Cathedral of Praise church staff, and they never seem to tire. When the people came to know Christ, the pastors and pastores (women pastors), the licensed church workers, go to those homes and they share Christ with the families as well. Five thousand more were added in the follow-up.

We stayed in a little hotel in Chinatown called the Lai Lai (which means come-come). Few of David's people have ever stayed in a hotel. Most of them, including David, don't own a car. At the crusades (the word they used instead of "concerts"), we did everything in English although Tagalog, a mixture of Spanish and Indonesian, is the official language. We sang at four different services the first Sunday at David's church. The next day we sang to 3,400 high school students in Manila, who were present for a special program.

Everything seemed to go wrong, and the sound system didn't work properly. I was grumbling to myself, saying, if this is the way it's going to be, we're in for a terrible time. Yet when we gave the invitation, seventeen hundred people came forward. I could hardly believe my eyes. I asked God to forgive my grumbling and lack of faith.

The next day we began to sing in the shopping centers. We did this regularly, four or five times daily. Every time we set up, we estimated crowds of somewhere between five thousand and seven thousand listened to us.

The church people roped off a big area in front of the stage for us to stand behind and present the gospel. Again I was unhappy. "Why don't you let the people come closer to the stage?"

"No, it's better this way," said one of the Filipino pastors.

"But they'll hear better—"

"Oh no, Pastor Roger, you wait. You see. You then understand why."

Oh, well, I thought, *I'm trying, but they just don't understand what we're doing.* I was thinking about the acoustics and about getting our music and our message across to more people. At the end of our meeting, one of the Filipino pastors gave the altar call.

Then I understood.

Every day, every time after we finished singing, hundreds of people surged forward. Had they not roped off the large space, there would have been no place for them to go. *Oh, God,* I said, *why do I always think I know best? Help me to do what I can do and leave the rest up to these Christians.*

I also quickly learned that Filipinos are very God-oriented people because of their strong Roman Catholic heritage. This made it so much easier to talk to them about Jesus.

While we had our wonderful times during the crusade, it still hurt to see the poverty. I watched individuals downtown in Manila urinate in the streets. Some slept on the sidewalk or took baths in the middle of the streets if they found water. Kids, seven or eight years old, walked around carrying infants and begging. I've never been around such poverty in all my life. And as is always true where there is such poverty, the military was evident everywhere. All stores (and also churches) have armed guards. The church people particularly warned us about the possibility of violence when we sang at PUP, the Polytechnic University of the Philippines. The leadership is communist.

"It'll be the toughest place you will sing because these are the students who marched on the U.S. embassy," David said. "They want the naval bases out of the Philippines." David Sumrall had scheduled one concert at PUP, and frankly I was frightened. So were the members of TRUTH. But because they needed to hear about Jesus Christ too, we didn't hesitate to go.

We had all been praying fervently for the students at PUP, and the Christians of Manila had been praying about this event for months. Extra security guards were visible because they didn't know how the students would respond to our white faces.

We set up that afternoon in the gym and tried to mingle with the people and make ourselves available; we tried to be careful as well. About five thousand students attended the concert. The only way I can explain the two hours we ministered is to call it a glorious concert. At the invitation a thousand students responded. In retrospect, it was probably the best of the thirty-seven concerts!

The results shouldn't have surprised us. Manila had been smothered in prayer. David Sumrall had trained two thousand volunteers. With them he had divided the city into sections, and they prayed for their city for nearly a year. In the States, we had spent almost a year praying about these crusades and asking the friends of TRUTH to join with us. And God answered our prayers. On our last Sunday at David's church we had 18,800 people in the services.

Everywhere we went the reception was more than we could ever have desired it to be. It was the finest response we have had in all our ministry. A highlight for us was witnessing the healings and miracles that took place. Not only were the people excited, but we were excited about what God was doing in the hearts of people.

We saw manifestations of God's power every day. Here are a few examples. On a Sunday morning, Mark Harris, our road director, was leading the service with TRUTH in a church outside Manila. Someone brought a woman in her late seventies; she was stooped, blind, and deaf. By the end of the service, not only had God given her a new heart, he had given her new hearing and sight, and she stood straight and even danced at the front.

On Wednesday evening, when a Filipino named Jay approached one of our trumpet players after a meeting, he asked, "Would you pray about my dad?" Among other things, he explained, "My father has been in the States for eight years, and I haven't heard from him in three years. I don't know if he's dead or what."

Several members of TRUTH prayed with Jay, asking God that the young man might hear something from his dad. Four days later we heard a knock on the prayer room door at the church. Jay motioned for one of our guys to come out. "I want to introduce you to my father," he said. Two days earlier, Jay's father had "just decided" he needed to go home.

Third, in a shopping center, a woman walked up, leaning on a cane. "I want prayer," she said, and before we had a chance to pray for her, she started praising God and threw away her cane. "I'm healed! I can walk!"

Here's a poignant story told to me by Gina Walker, one of the members of TRUTH: As we were setting up for one of the concerts at the marketplace, the largest outdoor shopping center in Manila, Gina noticed a little girl outside the stage area. Security guards flanked the space, but she leaned over the fence. She wasn't begging, just watching intently. She was the filthiest kid Gina had ever seen, with tattered clothing, no undergarments, her hair a mess—it probably had not been washed for weeks.

She was wearing flip-flop shoes five sizes too big for her. Gina felt drawn to the little girl. Even though we had all been told not to give the people money, Gina felt the Lord say, *You need to do something for this little girl. She is only one, but you can make a difference with one.*

Gina went over to her and tried to communicate, but the little girl spoke only Tagalog. Gina asked the security guard if he would interpret, and through him she asked, "Are these the only shoes you have to wear?" She nodded yes. As Gina and the little girl continued to talk, Gina learned that her name was Anna Lisa.

Just about that time, the concert was ready to start. "Wait!" Gina said. She ran up on the platform and hurriedly told the others about Anna Lisa and gathered what money they had. Most of them had a few pesos and were glad to give it. Two Christian girls whom I already knew and who both spoke English were standing near Anna Lisa. Gina asked them, "Would you do me a big favor, and take this little girl into the shopping center, and buy her some clothing?"

"What should we buy her?"

"Undergarments, a dress, shoes. You know. If there's anything left, something to eat and drink. Whatever there is enough money for."

"I shall be most happy to do this," one Christian girl said.

"Will you bring her back to me, please?" asked Gina.

"But of course we shall do that," said the other.

Gina gave one girl the money, and the other clasped Anna Lisa's hand and led the child down the street and into the store.

Half an hour later when we had a break between sets, Gina saw Anna Lisa running toward her. The little girl had run from the store all the way to the stage. She pushed right past the security guard, rushed up on the platform, and then stopped in front of Gina. She smiled and jumped up and down.

Anna Lisa didn't even look like the same little girl. She threw her arms around Gina and kept saying something over and over. Gina called one of the Christians over and asked her to interpret.

"She is saying that she loves you."

Nothing we did during our time there meant as much to Gina as that moment. Just seeing the little girl's face, and knowing that there might be a chance for her somewhere down the line because of what somebody had done for her, was just amazing to Gina.

None of Anna Lisa's family came to the concert. Gina wanted to take her home. She talked to one of the pastors and asked if she could walk Anna Lisa home.

"You had better not because you have to go on. The bus is waiting." Then she smiled, "But I will walk home with her."

Gina saw where Anna Lisa took the pastor because the child lived almost directly across the street, in a hut made of road signs. In that hovel lived Anna Lisa's parents, her grandmother, and a brother and sister. The pastor shared Jesus with the rest of the family, and they all accepted Christ as their personal Savior. For Gina Walker that was the best part.

We were told in our indoctrination period that we would see a lot of poverty, but, as in Brazil, we weren't to give any of the people money. We tried to abide by these instructions. But I have never been more pleased with a TRUTH member's heart to help than I was when I learned of Gina's compassionate gift to Anna Lisa—and its life-changing consequences.

The dedication of the church people never ceased to amaze me. They bought an old bus for us to travel in. They picked us up at seven o'clock some mornings; sometimes they kept us out until nine or ten at night so that we could hold concerts all day. Then they'd go back to the church and pray all night for the next day's services. At the end of the first week, I told TRUTH, "These people are better Christians than we are."

TRUTH didn't need me to tell them because they saw the commitment. One of them summed it up by saying, "They have nothing and give everything."

Chapter 11

A Painful Moment

Linda dialed 911. "I think my husband is having a heart attack," she said.

Through a fog of pain I heard her speaking. It felt as if a five-hundred-pound man was standing on my chest. The pressure was unlike anything I'd ever felt before.

In my misery I moaned, "My hands are tingling. My hands are tingling."

The strange tingling sensation in my hands continued, leading me to assume that I'd lost the circulation in them. I knew what that usually meant. *A heart attack*, I thought—*just like Dad*.

While I was growing up, I watched my dad have many such attacks, and I leaned in that same direction.

In our Tulsa hotel room, Linda had barely put down the phone when the paramedics knocked at the door. The ambulance happened to be passing by the hotel as Linda placed the call. The two men moved quickly and quietly. One of them took my vital signs, all the while asking me questions. The other sprayed nitroglycerin under my tongue, and the painful pressure eased somewhat.

As they were wheeling me out of the hotel on a gurney and taking me to the emergency room at the hospital, I didn't know if I was going to make it. I was in such pain at that moment that I didn't care very much either way.

My thoughts were racing through the pain. *This has come on me in just the last couple of days. It shouldn't be happening to me. Not now. I've just come back from vacation.*

Yet I had been tired two days earlier when I flew into Tulsa, Oklahoma, on Sunday, October 22, 1989. I had flown from Kansas City where we did our annual concert for Youth for Christ. I finally admitted to myself that I hadn't been feeling well for the past eight days. Nothing serious and no pain, just drained of energy.

Even worse was that I couldn't understand why I was so worn out. Linda and I had just returned from a week in London. Billy and his wife, Janet, had given us the trip for our twenty-fifth wedding anniversary. We loved London and had a wonderful time seeing so many places and eating a variety of foods.

Yet when we returned, both of us commented on being a little tired. Tired or not, immediately I started traveling again with TRUTH. Yet after a couple of days on the road with them, I needed to rest. I went home to Mobile where I stayed for the next eight days—days that should have been restful.

Instead of allowing myself total rest, however, I went into the office every day, talked on the phone, and handled a variety of business problems. Though I told myself that I was taking it easy, I had actually traded one kind of stress for another.

At the end of eight days, I started feeling restless and decided I wouldn't feel any worse on the road. Besides, I wanted to make the Kansas City concert, which is one of the best events of our year.

On October 21, the day of the concert, I was running a low-grade fever and still felt tired. *I'm not supposed to be tired,* I kept telling myself. *I had a vacation and eight days off afterward. I should be more energized than ever.* But I wasn't. I didn't feel well physically, and I didn't feel good about how the concert went, deciding that I had done a poor job of calling the concert (calling the order of songs).

The people who attend this event are wonderful; we always have a packed house with standing room only. Naturally I had wanted us to do our best. And it hadn't happened. Or at least it didn't happen for me. I may have been so worn out that I wouldn't have known if it did happen.

I went to bed early for a good night's rest. The next morning I flew to Tulsa for a concert. That night, immediately afterward, I went back to the hotel and straight to bed. On October 23, I had lunch with a cousin who lives in Tulsa.

By the time lunch was over, I knew something was definitely wrong. For the past few years I'd fought a recurring battle with diverticulitis in the lower part of my stomach—what some call "appendicitis of the left side." So I assumed that was my problem. When I have a diverticulitis flareup, I'm feverish, my stomach is tender to the touch, I'm a bit stooped, and I walk very slowly. I had all those symptoms, and yet this discomfort seemed different than before.

Previously whenever I became aware of an impending diverticulitis attack, I started being careful about what I ate, especially avoiding roughage, and I tried to get a lot of rest. *This is strange, I thought. I rested at home for over a week. For the last forty-eight hours I've been carefully watching my food. Yet I'm still miserable—and getting worse.*

Since St. Francis Hospital is across the street from the hotel where I was staying, I drove over to the emergency room as soon as lunch was over.

"I'm not feeling well," I said to the nurse behind the emergency room check-in. "I think my diverticulitis is acting up." After a long wait, I saw a doctor and described my symptoms. He gave me a shot to relieve the discomfort. And I did feel better.

I knew Linda had planned to fly from Mobile to Oklahoma City, where we would meet and then drive together to Oilton, Oklahoma. Our oldest son, John, was engaged to a lovely girl named Tracy Key, and we were supposed to go to Oilton for a concert and to meet her parents. Linda was in the Memphis Airport ready to board her plane to Oklahoma City when she got my message and immediately changed her itinerary.

I had already spent three and a half hours in the emergency room at the hospital, and I downplayed my symptoms to myself, refusing to think this could be anything more than another bout with diverticulitis. *I'll be fine,* I told myself. *I'll take the day off before we go to Oilton so I can be fully rested.*

Linda reached the hotel about four-thirty that afternoon. By then I wasn't getting better, but I tried to eat a light supper with her. After the medication wore off, I started going downhill. By five o'clock I felt worse than I had at noon. My hands started tingling and I frequently had to gasp for breath.

I tried to walk around the room, but that didn't help. I lay down, rolled over on one side, and then tried to rest on the other. I lay in every possible position, but I couldn't get any relief. As the moments ticked away, I grew sicker. The pressure on my chest increased, making me feel I couldn't breathe.

Linda immediately grabbed the phone and called 911.

At the hospital, I was held in the emergency room for another seven and a half hours, making it a total of ten and a half hours in the emergency room that day. Fortunately, this time I lay on a gurney, so I could relax.

Eventually an orderly wheeled me into one of the emergency rooms. I was wheeled down to x-ray, and nurses kept coming and going, giving me different tests, drawing blood, and checking my vital signs. I didn't care—I just hurt too much to feel involved with the action about me.

About midnight an orderly took me to a room. While I was at the hospital, they treated me for diverticulitis. The attending doctor, however, also suspected some problem with my heart. After four days, I didn't have any more signs of pressure in my chest, so I checked out and spent the night in the hotel.

The following morning, Linda and I flew back to Mobile. On the plane, after a long layover in Memphis, I started feeling pressure in my chest again. As soon as we landed at Mobile, Linda called our doctor.

"Take him to the Mobile Infirmary," Dr. Goldfarb said. Although not feeling as sick as I had in Tulsa, I was far from well. The heaviness on my chest was returning. Despite the pressure, I walked out to the airport entrance and got into the car. My son, John, drove us directly to the hospital. At the Mobile Infirmary, a nurse gave me something to ease the discomfort.

That evening, as I lay in the hospital bed, I kept thinking of one statement: *Come apart for awhile or come apart!*

Over and over the words came to me. *Come apart for awhile or come apart!* I knew only too well what they meant. One evening, after a concert in Louisville, Kentucky, my friend, Cec Murphey, looked right into my eyes and said, "Roger, you don't look very good; you look tired. I feel God has given me a word for you tonight: 'Come apart and rest awhile or come apart.'"

In the hospital I didn't remember the statement exactly, yet its meaning was becoming clearer. Two months earlier I had heard from God and had done nothing about it. That night I came to the conclusion that I had indeed come apart. "God, I'm sorry," I said. "Forgive me for not listening."

I stayed at the Mobile Infirmary for six days and, along with an ulcerated stomach, diverticulitis, colon and prostate trouble, innumerable tests, and medication for pain, I also had a heart catheterization. After the catheterization, however, my heart did seem to be in good shape. I finally asked Paul Goldfarb, who has been our family's doctor for thirty years, "How do I describe to people what's wrong with me?"

Dr. Goldfarb, who thinks that I'm absolutely crazy because of the way I travel and live, said, "After nineteen years on the road you're a mess; consequently, your stomach is a mess. Roger, you have to change your lifestyle."

I immediately followed his advice. I dropped a few pounds. I now try to watch what I eat. I've even given up carbonated drinks. I'm trying to decide on the right exercise program for me.

~

After four days in Tulsa at St. Francis and six days in the Mobile Infirmary, after being poked, probed, and pricked, I said to Dr. Goldfarb, "Surely they don't have any more needles here. Even if they do, I don't have any more blood. Isn't it time for me to go home?" He laughed, but he agreed; he signed my release.

For the next seven weeks I remained, as I call it, "on the shelf." I didn't do anything; I couldn't because I had no energy. Gradually I improved. In early December I went back on the road for a couple of weeks. I learned quickly that I could do fine for three days. On the fourth, I'd crash and be without much energy. I'd never been that way before.

When I work, I throw myself fully into what I'm doing, and I don't know how to hold back on my energy. During those weeks of being on the shelf, TRUTH worked for seven weeks without me. They also did very well. Mark Harris, our capable road director, was in charge, and he did an outstanding job. I missed our annual California tour and the Colorado tour, which are important to us.

For years I had tried to instill in the group that they could do all right without my always having to be there. They proved me correct. After I had been home for six weeks, however, a serious and emergency situation erupted in California. "This needs my immediate attention," I said to Linda. "I'm going to fly out there tomorrow."

"Oh no, Roger," she said, "you can't. You're not up to it."

"They need me. I've got to go."

"You can't go! Dr. Goldfarb said you shouldn't leave town until he tells you. What happens if you get sick out there?"

"God will just have to take care of me," I said. "I've got to go. TRUTH needs me."

"Let Mark and the other leaders take care of it. He's done a good job so far—"

"This is different. This is something that only I can take care of."

"You're really not well enough." Linda stared straight at me and said, "And you know it."

Even though I knew she was probably right, I felt I must go, regardless of my health. I honestly believed that I was the only person who could straighten out the delicate situation.

Linda has known me for a long time. She understands how I feel about being responsible for TRUTH. But she was worried about me too. Tears filled her eyes as she said, "You're still too weak and too sick. I don't think you could handle the flight, let alone have any energy to straighten out anything."

"I have to go, Linda. I have to."

"Then I'm going with you."

"No," I said, "it's something I have to do alone. I know I can't get out there and do the concert," I said, "but I can be their leader long enough to go through this crisis with them."

By then I had been at home more than four weeks; I was tired of lying around, tired of being ill, and I wanted to be back on the road—where I'd been for almost twenty years.

"I'm not going to argue and get you more upset," Linda said finally. She brushed away her tears. "I'm going upstairs to read my Bible and pray."

Linda and I seldom argue. This time she was so upset that I would consider making such a long trip that she couldn't talk anymore. I was hurt over her attitude, convinced that she simply hadn't grasped either the seriousness of the situation or my need to be there as the only one who could handle the turmoil.

Our son John came in minutes later. To my surprise, when he heard about the crisis TRUTH faced, he sided with his mother. "Don't do it," he said.

"I have to," I answered. "It's my responsibility." Like his mother, John put up the same arguments. As I listened, I decided that even with both of them questioning me, I must go to California.

After John left, I felt totally alone. *Oh, God, doesn't anybody understand? Why can't they see that I have to do this? Can't you make them understand how serious the problem is?*

While I had heard what John said and what Linda had told me and tried to be objective about the situation, I just couldn't see any other way. It was a critical situation, and big problems had already erupted.

Later, Linda and I talked about it one more time. To pacify her more than for any other reason, I said, "Okay, Linda, I'll do this. I'll wait another twenty-four hours. If the situation hasn't been resolved by then, I'm going out."

She didn't argue. Maybe the finality of my tone made it clear that I intended to go. I also knew that Linda was praying fervently during that period. To my total surprise, within twenty-four hours the situation had resolved itself!

Quite simply, the people in charge exercised decisive leadership, and almost immediately everything functioned normally again. Even more amazing, they handled the problem exactly the way I would have handled it!

Twenty-four hours later—the very time when I would have flown to California—I had a relapse. I felt almost as sick as I had when I came home from the Mobile Infirmary. "Thanks, God," I said, "for preventing me from going." I also thanked Linda and John for standing their ground and told them, "You were right."

As a leader I've said many times to TRUTH that time is a friend and that time heals a lot of wounds. My rushing out to California would have violated one of the important lessons I had wanted them to learn. From where I was, though, I could think only about asserting myself as the director and fixing it.

So Roger Breland learned one of his own lessons: Sometimes waiting is best because time is a friend.

During my seven weeks on the shelf, I wasn't much good at the office. Though I was glad to be helpful to the family, I was not any good for TRUTH—and probably was not much good for me. I didn't contribute; I was just there. I don't think I wanted to contribute. On the road, I could depend on Mark and on our two key people in the office, Billy and Greg. At home I could rely on Linda as I had always been able to do. During that period I closed the door emotionally. I didn't feel like doing anything while I was waiting to feel better. I didn't want to do anything; I was completely unmotivated—totally unlike my normal self.

On one of my follow-up visits, Dr. Goldfarb looked me over and said, "Roger, you're depressed. Why are you so depressed?"

"Am I?" I tried to laugh it off. I hadn't even thought about being depressed, but he was right.

"Well you are depressed and we can do something to help." He prescribed antidepressants. Within days my attitude began to change.

In early December, at the beginning of our Christmas tour, I started to feel more like myself again. I went back on the road, and it felt good to be active again. I assumed my role, not only as the leader of the group, but also as a performer in the concerts.

After I had passed through this whole ordeal, I sensed that many people expected me to share with them some great pearl of spiritual awareness. And they asked, "Roger, what did you learn from this? What did God teach you? What new insight did you receive?" No great new insight or truth came out of this time on the shelf. I was just tired and sick and needed complete rest.

In all honesty, I was too tired and too sick to think about anything. It was just a miserable time for me. I was still several weeks away from being able to do what I needed to do physically. I had to face that I was mentally, physically, musically, and spiritually drained. All these interrelated areas of my life hit bottom at the same time. I'd been sick before, had even been hospitalized, but I'd never undergone anything like this—and for such a lengthy period. I'll long remember October and November of 1989 as painful, difficult moments. I had no energy to search for a lovely moment. Not then anyway.

I had started on the road when I was twenty-seven. I turned forty-six in December. That birthday and the sickness forced me to admit the reality that my body no longer responds the way it used to.

Even now, I'm a little more winded after walking the length of the Atlanta Airport than I was ten years ago. The Memphis Airport is even worse. This also means I have to learn to depend more on my people and less on myself.

Right now I feel confident that TRUTH could survive without me, but there was a time when I didn't, especially when I felt insecure about my own leadership ability. In those early days I was running scared, not knowing if we'd survive on the road as a group. Although I believed God had called me to lead

TRUTH, I had a deep fear that if I didn't give every ounce of strength and commitment, we'd fall apart.

Periodically we still face problems and crises in TRUTH. For example, we've had a young man named Mark Harris with us for four years. He's going to leave, along with three of our male singers. They're going out to form a group called 4Him. We're proud of all four, we wish them the best, and I don't see how we can survive without them. Yet at the same time, I know that TRUTH will survive. We'll recruit new singers, and raise up other leaders even while we still miss people like Mark a lot.

Though I know that TRUTH can survive without me, I'm also aware of a significant problem. I was a minister of music and hosted a lot of people for years. I've grown sensitive to those who want (sometimes demand) the leader to be present. In one sense I am TRUTH—the one consistent factor in our nearly twenty-year history. During my time on the shelf, I thought about those people who would be unhappy if I weren't present. Some might even feel insulted.

Yet I learned that I can't be there all the time. TRUTH does more than three hundred concerts a year, which is demanding enough. The larger we grow, the more business matters we have to handle, and those consume my time and energy as well. We don't just drive across the state, but we travel halfway around the world, responding to the vision God has given us to bear witness in foreign lands. The preparation for TRUTH is more demanding than ever before.

Beyond my ministry, I have responsibilities to my wife and to my sons. But probably the hardest lesson of this experience is learning that I have a responsibility to take care of Roger.

~

Yes, those weeks were a painful moment for me, for Linda, for our family, and for TRUTH. But I now see more clearly: God was working behind the curtain. As I look back and see God's tender, teaching hand over this painful time, I can say, "Even that moment had its loveliness."

Future Moments

How thankful I am for the open doors around the world!

At this present time we are planning, praying, and preparing for a '91 Spring tour to Russia, Romania, and Hungary. We will be singing concerts in the universities and sports arenas. Our Russian friends have requested that we bring Bibles and wheelchairs.

Unsolicited invitations have poured into our office the past few months. Some of those include Barcelona, Spain in conjunction with the 1992 Summer Olympics, Egypt, Colombia, Brazil, Chile, Australia, and New Zealand.

Our most recent overseas trip to the Philippines, Singapore, and India was postponed due to the unrest in Manila. We hope and pray to return to the Philippines.

There are many new faces in the current TRUTH. It is exciting and overwhelming what God is doing in the hearts and lives of all of us. It is as if the Spirit of God is sweeping through our midst. Tears have flowed as repentance and confession of sin is heard. God seems to be purifying us so He can fill and anoint us with His power for the great task in the days ahead.

So many dear ones keep asking, "Roger, how do

you do it? How much longer?" I am seriously and prayerfully asking myself and God these questions. As always, TRUTH is so blessed with capable leaders. God is teaching me that He can work through TRUTH without me. I am stubbornly learning that I must take better care of this body that has traveled so many miles.

My three sons love God, their dad, and TRUTH in that order. I believe God will use one, two if not all three of them in our ministry one day. What more could a dad ask for?

It's been said, "that the light that shines the brightest at home shines the farthest."

For whatever has been accomplished for God's Kingdom at home and beyond, we give God all the glory.

Epilogue

The most delightful change in my life since the original publishing date of 1991 is that I have become a proud grandfather of four! Please look for the pictures. By the way, Linda and I love being grandparents!

The first grand-daughter arrived September 8, 1992 — Elizabeth Rose. She lovingly calls me Grandpa and Linda, Nana. My ears have never heard sweeter words.

Weddings abounded in the Breland family in 1995 and early 1996. Jeremy married Jennifer Blomstrom of Hershey, Pennsylvania in June 1995. Amy Thames of Augusta, Georgia became Jason's wife in January 1996.

God had already blessed with my first daughter, Tracy, John's wife. Amy and Jennifer are no exception. These three daughters are the daughters I always wanted. Each loves Jesus, my sons, Linda and me. For this I am very thankful.

In May 1995 a very special second grand-daughter was born, Caroline Olivia. She is a little angel sent from God. I love her so much.

As I am writing this, Linda and I are on our way to see and hold for the very first time our newborn twins...John Roger III and Anna Victoria.

John and Tracy had some difficulties in having children. One morning as Linda prayed for them she wrote their names and the date December 31, 1991 by this verse, Psalm 113:9, "He makes the barren woman abide in the house. As a joyful mother of children." Praise the Lord! God has been so good.

My final words in this book were concerning my three

sons. God has allowed all of them to work with me at this moment in time. What an awesome privilege for me. Jason is a vocalist and the road director doing the concerts in my absence. John and Jeremy book several Christian artists including TRUTH and promote concerts. Their company is The Breland Group. To say we enjoy working together is an understatement.

I am trusting God with each son and his wife. Linda and I are praying daily for His will, plan and purpose to be accomplished in them...for God to cause all things to work together for good and for His Kingdom to come and His will be done in their hearts and in their families.

In 1991 I was approached by my friend, Mike Coleman, the founder and President of Integrity Music. He was the drummer for The Varsity in the Spring Hill days. He sighed TRUTH as an artist and we have completed five recording projects. These include several #1 songs, "Givin' It Up", "God Is In Control", "Wings Like Eagles", "Mind of Christ", and the most requested and used of God, "If You Could See Me Now." It was written by former TRUTH vocalist Kim Noblitt for my sister, Debby, after her husband, Jeff, went to be with the Lord in March 1992. This song was nominated for "Song of the Year" for two consecutive years. It was the song of the year for many as it encouraged and helped thousands who had lost loved ones.

Eastern Europe has been TRUTH's mission focus and destination for three trips in the past five years. An entire book could be written about those experiences, what God is doing there and how He continues changing all of us in the process. Our first two were concert tours to Moscow, Russia, Budapest, Hungary and Romania. In Oradea, Romania, TRUTH worked with Pastor Peter Vidu and assisted in the raising of funds to help build a sanctuary. What an incredible blessing to know there are such saints on this earth! They have nothing and give everything. They are like Jesus.

This past year we joined forces with Slavic Gospel Association to help the "Children of Chernobyl." On our most recent trip, the TRUTH vocalists and I visited an orphanage, a clinic, a hospital, and a prison in Minsk, Belarus. In TRUTH's Christmas concerts we invited Americans to send a package to these Russian prisoners and hundreds responded.

God is teaching me that when we meet others needs then God meets our needs through others. Philippians 4:19 says, "And my God shall supply all your needs according to His riches in glory in Christ Jesus."

I have a vision for TRUTH to help meet the spiritual and physical needs of the world...especially in Russia. Invitations have been received to Mexico, Nicaragua, and China. As God leads and opens doors, TRUTH will go.

God had met some of our transportation needs in 1995. Through the gifts of two men God provided us with a much needed new trailer. In January 1996, our brand new beautiful 45 foot bus was delivered. An absolute miracle made possible by the many gifts both small and great of God's people. Every gift was deeply appreciated.

Our remaining transportation need is for a new truck to pull our trailer. The present one is tired and under-powered.

One of my greatest joys these 25 years has been to stand by and watch very proudly those who step off the TRUTH bus. Three dynamic ministries were launched from TRUTH during the last five years. These were 4-Him, Alicia, and Karen-Leigh.

A significant date — August 8-11, 1996 in Nashville, Tennessee, we will all converge to celebrate twenty-five years of TRUTH. What we will joyfully celebrate is God's faithfulness and help — giving Him the glory for all these years and trusting Him for our future.

The past year of 1995 was another one of those most difficult years. Linda and I have been agreeing in prayer to hear God's voice and to really know His will and His purpose concerning TRUTH'S ministry — present and future. He has spoken to us. God's word for TRUTH all these years has never changed. He has brought us back to the very basics — the verse in I Thessalonians 2:4, "But just as we have been approved by God to be entrusted with the gospel, so we speak, not as pleasing men but God, who examines our hearts."

As I have reflected on these moments from the recent years of TRUTH, I find my life continues to be filled with lovely moments. And the search goes on...

MY TRIBUTE (TO GOD BE THE GLORY)
By: Andraé Crouch
1971 by Lexicon Music, Inc.

How can I say thanks
for the things You have done for me?
Things so undeserved,
yet You give to prove Your love for me.
The voices of a million angels
could not express my gratitude;
All that I am and ever hope to be,
I owe it all to Thee.

To God be the glory;
To God be the glory,
To God be the glory
for the things He has done.
With His blood
He has saved me,
With His power
He has raised me,
To God be the glory
for the things He has done.

Just let me live my life,
let it be pleasing, Lord, to thee;
And should I gain any praise,
Let it go to Calvary.
With His blood
He has saved me,
With His power
He has raised me,
To God be the glory
For the things he has done.

Write to:
Roger Breland
c/o TRUTH
P.O. Box 9459
Mobile, AL 36691